Flannery O'Connor

By DOROTHY WALTERS
Wichita State University

TWAYNE PUBLISHERS
A DIVISION OF G. K. HALL & CO., BOSTON

Library of Congress Catalog Card Number: 72-934
ISBN 0-8057-0556-2

MANUFACTURED IN THE UNITED STATES OF AMERICA

Contents

About the Author

Dorothy Walters holds a Ph.D. from the University of Oklahoma (1960) and has taught at the University of Colorado and Wichita State University, where she is now Associate Professor of English. Her major field of interest is twentieth-century literature, with special emphasis on the literature of Ireland, the literature of the American South, and literature written by women. She taught the first course in women writers at Wichita State, and has present co-taught the course "Women in Society."

Preface

Flannery O'Connor said of her work, "the look of this fiction is going to be wild . . . it is almost of necessity going to be violent and comic, because of the discrepancies it seeks to combine." [1] Many readers, confronted for the first time by these wild discrepancies, come away with a sense of having undergone some overpowering psychological experience but remain unsure as to its ultimate meaning or cause. This book aims to reveal, as nearly as possible, the sources of that power and the meaning of its expression. O'Connor's deep religious commitment, her skillful employment of comic machinery, her subtle use of recurrent symbol and image all provide rich fields for investigation, but none alone accounts for the ultimate impact of work upon reader. Individually, each story moves close to a perfect realization of its own ideal intention, but her total work is also impressive in its overall coherence, and a study of the whole serves to illuminate by cross-reflection the meaning of the individual parts. Ostensible simplicity is attained through the manipulation of complex— frequently antithetic—modes, and to these one must turn in order to grasp the sources of her creative strength and the nature of her artistic achievement.

I begin with a look at O'Connor's life as the source of much of her art, suggesting how her background provided an apparent source for some of her most obvious features—her Southernness, her Catholicism, her persistent irony, her preoccupation with death. Next, I present a fairly detailed discussion of the "method" —the specific "blend" of disparates which gives the O'Connor work its peculiar stamp of originality. Essentially, these are the antinomies of tragic and comic modes, fused in a vision which is predominantly Christian but which carries pronounced undertones of something quite dissimilar. I then show how the coherence of method and perspective permits a grouping of the works under a limited number of thematic categories.

For the benefit of readers primarily interested in particular works, I have treated each of the nineteen early collected stories individually. I have arranged these into relevant groupings, studying them under such aspects as the reliance upon catastrophe as a weapon to yield salvation or judgement; the sacramental center from which her vision radiates; the moment of grace; and the various convergences—spiritual, racial, and social—which send recurrent shocks through her created world. The two novels— *Wise Blood* and *The Violent Bear It Away*—are discussed in separate chapters. In them O'Connor explores diverse paths to salvation, one through the way of atonement (passive), the other through the avenue of involvement (active). In the final chapter, I note the ways in which she is allied with the "tradition" of Southern literature, as well as with some of the major impulses of twentieth-century world literature, and I suggest how she transcends both her region and her era to take her place among the timeless orders of the true artist.

Flannery O'Connor, speaking of her vocation, observed that the writer is one who "keeps going deeper and deeper." So it is with the reader of her stories. One pentrates many levels, only to arrive at the verge of "mystery" which, by her own definition, is "what is left after everything else has been explained." With a full awareness of the unexplainable mystery which reposes at the heart of her imagined universe, I discuss those areas which are perhaps "explainable," in the hope that thereby the reader will be better equipped to take his own journey into those wordless regions where her final meaning resides.

I wish to express deep gratitude to Professors Regina Barnett, Margaret Haley, Nancy Millett, Mary Elizabeth Nelson, and Marilyn Sawin, all of whom read the manuscript and offered valuable comment; to Professor Robert Fitzgerald, who graciously spoke with me during a busy schedule in Denver; to Anne Branscombe, who shared with me her reminiscences of Milledgeville; to Professor Donna Gerstenberger, who was in a real sense the instigator of the project; to Regina O'Connor, who kindly answered my questions concerning her daughter; and to the University of Colorado Council on Creative Research, which supplied funds and time for most of the writing of the book.

Acknowledgments

Quotations from *Wise Blood, The Violent Bear It Away, Everything That Rises Must Converge,* and *Mystery and Manners* are by permission of Farrar, Straus & Giroux. Quotations from *A Good Man Is Hard to Find and Other Stories* are by permission of Harcourt, Brace Jovanovich.

Chronology

1925   Mary Flannery O'Connor born March 25 in Savannah, Georgia, to Edward F. O'Connor, Jr., and Regina (Cline) O'Connor.

1938   Moved with mother and father to Milledgeville, Georgia.

1941   Father died, February 1.

1942   Graduated from Peabody High School, Milledgeville.

1942–   Attended Georgia State College for Women (now Georgia
1945   Woman's College), Milledgeville, graduating in 1945.

1945–   Attended Writer's Workshop, State University of Iowa
1948   (now University of Iowa); Master of Fine Arts, 1947. "The Geranium" published in *Accent*, summer, 1946.

1948–   Brief residence at Yaddo. "The Capture" published *Made-*
1949   *moiselle;* "Train" (from *Wise Blood*), in *Sewanee Review*.

1949   Lived in New York City. "The Woman on the Stairs" (later titled "A Stroke of Good Fortune"), published in *Tomorrow;* "The Heart of the Park" and "The Peeler" (both from *Wise Blood*), in *Partisan Review*.

1949–   Lived with Sally and Robert Fitzgerald in Connecticut;
1950   first major attack of lupus in December, 1950.

1951   From this year on, lived with mother on farm near Milledgeville.

1952   *Wise Blood* published.

1953   Kenyon Review Fellowship.

1954   Reappointed Kenyon Fellow. "The Life You Save May Be Your Own" won second prize, O. Henry awards.

1955   *A Good Man Is Hard to Find* published. "A Circle in the Fire" won second prize, O. Henry awards.

1956   First of several lecture trips to colleges and universities.

1957   National Institute of Arts and Letters grant. "Greenleaf" won first prize, O. Henry awards.

1958   Traveled to Lourdes and Rome with mother. Audience with pope.

1959 Ford Foundation grant.
1960 *The Violent Bear It Away.*
1962 Honorary Doctor of Letters, St. Mary's College, Notre Dame.
1963 Honorary Doctor of Letters, Smith College. "Everything That Rises Must Converge" won first prize, O. Henry awards.
1964 Died August 3 in Milledgeville hospital. "Revelation" won first prize, O. Henry awards.
1965 *Everything That Rises Must Converge.*
1971 *The Complete Stories of Flannery O'Connor* won National Book Award.

CHAPTER *1*

A Milledgeville Girl

IN its external features, the life of Flannery O'Connor is easily told. Born in Savannah, Georgia, to a Catholic family, she grew up in Milledgeville. She attended the local woman's college and later the Iowa Writer's Workshop,[1] and she lived briefly with Sally and Robert Fitzgerald in Connecticut. When she was twenty-five, she suffered her first major attack of disseminated lupus, the disease which would bring her death fourteen years later.[2] From 1951 on, she lived with her mother at Andalusia, a farm near Milledgeville; she continued to write but at a steadily decreasing rate. Fortunately, her talents matured early; and, though her total output was relatively small, her achievement is impressive. Indeed, Evelyn Waugh found it difficult to believe that a girl in her twenties could have produced the stunning effects of the early stories, observing: "If this is the unaided work of a young lady it is a remarkable product." [3]

Such, briefly, are the surface features of Flannery O'Connor's life. To glimpse more closely the person *behind* the public record, we must probe beyond "fact" to more significant levels of meaning.

I *Two Ways of Looking at a Peacock*

Of the many traits which distinguish Flannery O'Connor as a personality and as a writer, none is more striking than her remarkable capacity to blend the *comic* and the *serious* in a single view of reality. This dual perspective, evident throughout her work, characterizes her life response from her early years. In particular, it is reflected in her attitude toward three subjects which were of special concern to her: peacocks, cartoon drawings, and her own prolonged illness.

O'Connor was from childhood fascinated by birds of various kinds. At the age of five, she owned a chicken with a unique talent: it could walk both forward and backward. Pathé News sent a cameraman to record the bizarre phenomenon, and O'Connor insisted that this event marked the high point of her life, for everything after that came as an anticlimax. Later, while taking a required high school course in home economics, she was given the assignment of making a garment suitable for a small child relative. On the day the class was to exhibit its achievements, O'Connor arrived leading in tow not a child but a chicken, which was nattily attired in a white piqué coat with a stylishly belted back.[4]

Flannery O'Connor's interest in fowl continued undiminished in later life. In an article in *Holiday Magazine* (September, 1961), entitled "Living with a Peacock," she explains that, although she owned "a pen of pheasants and a pen of quail, a flock of turkeys, seventeen geese, a tribe of mallard ducks, three Japanese silky bantams, two Polish Crested ones, and several chickens of a cross between these last and the Rhode Island Red," she nonetheless "felt a lack." That lack was filled when she answered an advertisement in the Florida *Market Bulletin* for three-year-old peafowl.

Commenting on the aloof attitude of these creatures, she observes: "Over the years their attitude toward me has not grown more generous. If I appear with food, they condescend, when no other way can be found, to eat it from my hand; if I appear without food, I am just another object. If I refer to them as 'my' peafowl, the pronoun is legal, nothing more. I am the menial, at the beck and squawk of any feathered worthy who wants service." The peacock is, she explains, an extremely fickle bird; indeed, no amount of coaxing can cause him to lift his tail unless he is so moved. But, once the impressive event occurs, most witnesses are properly awed by the glory spread before them. Not all, however, are so favorably impressed. One telephone repairman, having waited impatiently for some time, was at last rewarded by the sight of the magnificent elevation. The workman's response was unexpected: " 'Never saw such long ugly legs,' the man said. 'I bet that rascal could outrun a bus.' "

O'Connor, although she is fully alert to the comic aspects of this impressive creature, is also deeply aware of the more serious aspect of his character: in "The Displaced Person," the peacock becomes the central—religious—symbol; for the bird is associated with his traditional role as the emblem of Christ. The priest, gaz-

ing at the "tiers of small pregnant suns [which] floated in a green-
gold haze over his head," exclaims in awe, "Christ will come like
that."

At the conclusion of the *Holiday* piece, O'Connor relates a
curious dream which suggests that she herself closely identified
with the splendid bird: "Lately I have had a recurrent dream.
I am five years old and a peacock. A photographer has been sent
from New York and a long table is laid in celebration. The meal
is to be an exceptional one: myself. I scream, 'Help! Help!'—and
awaken." This account—though ostensibly humorous—carries
subtle suggestions of a more serious nature. Given O'Connor's
employment of the peacock in its full symbolic role as the emblem
of Christ at the Second Coming in "The Displaced Person," and
in view of her own consistent equation of the role of the writer
with that of the religious prophet, it seems valid to interpret the
dream as a disguised ceremony of the Eucharist at which the
sacrifice of the artist-Christ (herself) is being celebrated. The
dream, with its identification of self with sacrificial symbol,
projects the major aspects of her own view of the writer's role:
the divine origin of his talent (". . . whatever his initial gift is,
it comes from God")[5] and the self-sacrifice which the pursuit of
his "vocation" necessarily entails.

A second interest that reflects her serious-comic point of view
is cartooning. Noted for her ability as a cartoonist even in high
school, as a college undergraduate O'Connor contributed a weekly
sketch to the campus newspaper, and, in fact, did a cartoon mural
for the student union building.[6] Her evident talent in this direction led many of her friends to predict for her a career as a professional cartoonist.

The method of the cartoonist is closely allied to that employed
by O'Connor in her writing. Cartoons characteristically make a
serious statement through ostensibly comic means, using exaggera-
tion and emphasis to achieve their effects. The swift stroke,
the telling detail—these quickly sketch the significant features of
the subject. O'Connor is a master of the instant characterization
through the potent phrase: ladies "dressed like parrots" or a train
conductor with a face like "an ancient bloated bull dog" have
their intrinsic natures well defined even before they speak. Even
the major characters of O'Connor have certain "cartoon" qualities,
for their *essential* traits are delineated in absolutely sharp out-

lines. All superfluities are removed to focus on the stark profiles of the rigidly drawn figures. Finally, the satiric cartoon permits the artist to make his comment about the world through *distance* and *indirection*. The comment is *implicit* in the portrayal, for the creator, though in control, is invisible. Again, this unvarying method of Flannery O'Connor is found throughout her fiction.

Toward her physical debility O'Connor maintained a public attitude of amused detachment, remarking: "The disease is of no consequence to my writing, since for that I use my head and not my feet." [7] Commenting on her restricted daily schedule, she noted: "I write from nine to twelve, and spend the rest of the day recuperating from it." [8] In a letter to her friend Richard Stern (1959), she offered a mock-pathetic description of her typical daily activities: "This is the season at which I pick up peafowl feathers as the dear birds shed. In the cool of the evening I am to be seen out in the pasture, bending painfully from my two aluminum sticks, reaching for some bright feather. I hope that this affecting picture touches you." [9]

Despite the seeming offhand irony with which she was able to view her condition, the record of those years of illness indicates a seriously reduced productivity. She never openly complains of her illness; but, in a letter to Stern (1964), she laments: "All I've written this year have been a few letters." [10] In an earlier missive (1963), she had "chided" Stern for his prolific literary output, but her bantering tone barely disguises her own poignant envy: "What are you fixing to do, publish another novel? Do you want to be known as One-a-year Stern? I am doing my best to create the impression it takes 7 years to write a novel. The four-hour week. You are not helping the Brotherhood. Examine your conscience. Think. Meditate. Shilly-shally." [11]

Flannery O'Connor was able to laugh in the gravest of circumstances. However, her own illness—as well as her father's early death—suggests an obvious source of a pervasive concern of her writing: omnipresent death and disaster. Her work is filled with depictions of violence, annihilation, the somber moment of the final crisis. She attributed her preoccupation to her religious background: "I'm a born Catholic and death has always been brother to my imagination. I can't imagine a story that doesn't properly end in it or in its foreshadowings." [12] "In every story there is some minor revelation which, no matter how funny the story may be, gives us a hint of the unknown, of death." [13] This pervasive awareness of death as the inescapable fact of existence charges her work with a powerful tension and places her in the line of the great tragic writers, who have ever insisted that man's own mortality is the central feature of all human experience. Symbol, method, subject—all reflect the capacity of O'Connor to view life simultaneously in its comic and tragic aspects. The dual vision of the life becomes the characteristic approach in the art.

II   *The Writer as Southern Catholic*

When Flannery O'Connor was asked to name the crucial influences upon her life, she answered: "Probably . . . being a Catholic, and a Southerner, and a writer." [14]

O'Connor's identity as a Southerner provided her with the materials from which she shaped her vision. Milledgeville itself had been the capital of Georgia before the "War Between the States"; the Cline mansion, purchased by her maternal grandfather in 1886, was for a time the governor's residence. O'Connor was fully exposed to the Southern milieu, with its well-known tendency to glamorize the achievements of the past and to resist the problems of the present. The familiar Southern types, spanning the entire range of the social scale from illiterate laborer to backwoods preacher to nostalgic pseudoaristocrat; the authentic cadences of Southern speech, with its own peculiar types and variations; the regional settings, typically rural with occasional shifts into the city, although the metropolis itself is liberally infused with provincial elements—these mark her unmistakably as a "Southern" writer, who depicts a clearly recognizable region with its own essential features and attributes.

Speaking of the specific impress which the South makes upon its inhabitants, she said: "The things we see, hear, smell, and touch affect us long before we believe anything at all. The South impresses its image on the Southerner—be he Catholic or not— from the moment he is able to distinguish one sound from another. He takes it in through his ears and hears it again in his own voice; and by the time he is capable of using his imagination for fiction, he finds that his senses respond to a certain reality that he may or may not be able to tolerate." [15]

Her Southernness is undeniable, but, as with the other major writers who have emerged from the area, the region is for her an instrument, not an end. She herself was acutely aware of the dangers of lapsing into a restrictive "regionalism": "In almost every hamlet you'll find at least one lady writing epics in Negro dialect and probably two or three old gentlemen who have impossible historical novels on the way. The woods are full of regional writers, and it is the great horror of every serious Southern writer that he will become one of them." [16] Those Southern writers who have succeeded in eluding the trap of provincialism have done so by imposing on the local materials a larger vision which carries the immediate happenings into universal, mythic levels. For Flannery O'Connor, the myth is specifically Christian.

O'Connor was born into a family with a long tradition of Catholic identification on both sides. The first mass said in Milledgeville took place in her great-grandfather's hotel room; the local Catholic church stands on ground originally donated by another ancestor. Her personal commitment was intense. Fitzgerald notes that in Connecticut she attended mass daily. And by her bedside on the Georgia farm were three books: a breviary, a Sunday missal, and a Bible. The extent of her conviction is reflected in her comment on the Eucharist: "If it were only a symbol, I'd say to hell with it." [17]

O'Connor's faith commitment is total. She insists that the event by which all subsequent human action must be measured is the agony of Christ on the Cross: "For I am no disbeliever in spiritual purpose and no vague believer. I see from the standpoint of Christian orthodoxy. This means that for me the meaning of life is centered in our Redemption by Christ and what I see in the world I see in its relation to that. I don't think that this is a position that can be taken half-way or one that is particularly easy in these times to make transparent in fiction." [18]

Her Catholic heritage thus furnished a stable moral perspective from which she consistently views her subjects. This is not to imply, however, that her work lacks relevance for the non-Catholic or even for the non-Christian audience. Her faith must be understood to decipher her meanings, but not, I think, necessarily accepted in full—any more than we are obliged to endorse the theological positions of Dante or of Milton in order to share their esthetic visions or comprehend their meaning. Basically, her message is ecumenical rather than restrictive. Her concern is with the age-old issues of sin and salvation, the pervasive apathy and pride which sap the spirit of man in the secular city, and the transcendent visions which prepare the break from moral sloth to active belief. She noted: "I will admit to certain preoccupations with belief and with death and grace and the devil." [19] But such concerns are widespread.

O'Connor insisted that the writer's commitment to an established set of beliefs serves as a source of freedom, not restraint:

> I have heard it said that belief in Christian dogma is a hindrance to the writer, but I myself have found nothing further from the truth. Actually, it frees the storyteller to observe. It is not a set of rules which fixes what he sees in the world. It affects his writing primarily by guaranteeing his respect for mystery. [20]
>
> A belief in fixed dogma cannot fix what goes on in life or blind the believer to it. It will, of course, add a dimension to the writer's observation which many cannot, in conscience, acknowledge exists, but as long as what they *can* acknowledge is present in the work, they cannot claim that any freedom has been denied the artist. A dimension taken away is one thing, a dimension added is another. . . . [21]

O'Connor described the writer's function in religious terminology: the key words are "vocation," "prophecy," and "judgment." Writing itself is seen as a "vocation" in the religious sense of the term. A sacred calling, the gift of the writer is derived from a divine source:

> This [the writer's task] is first of all a matter of vocation, and a vocation is a limiting factor which extends even to the kind of material that the writer is able to apprehend imaginatively. The writer can choose what he writes about but he cannot choose what he is able to make live, and so far as he is concerned, a living deformed character is acceptable and a dead whole one is not. The Christian writer particularly will feel that whatever his initial gift is, it comes from God; and no matter how minor a gift it is, he will not be willing to destroy it by trying to use it outside its proper limits. [22]

The writer's proper role is that of "prophet." As prophet, he performs a dual function: "There is the prophetic sense of 'seeing through' reality and there is also the prophetic function of re-calling people to known but ignored truths." [23] The fiction writer should be characterized not by his predictive capacity but by his perceptive vision: "His kind of vision is prophetic vision. Proph-ecy, which is dependent on the imagination and not the moral faculty, need not be a matter of predicting the future. In the novelist's case, it is a matter of seeing near things with their extensions of meaning and thus of seeing far things close up. The prophet is the realist of distances, and it is this kind of realism that goes into great novels." [24]

The artist's responsibility embraces not only prophecy but "judgment":

> I think the novelist does more than just show how a man feels. I think he also makes a judgment on the value of that feeling. It may not be an overt judgment. Probably it will be sunk in the work but it is there because, in the good novel, judgment is not separated from vision.[25]

> In the greatest fiction, the writer's moral sense coincides with his dramatic sense, and I see no way for it to do this unless his moral judgment is part of the very act of seeing, and he is free to use it.[26]

III *An Austere Angel*

A background both Southern and Catholic, a view of the artist grounded on a firm moral base, an extreme sensitivity to the mixed tragicomic nature of experience—these are the forces which shape O'Connor's vision and lend color and direction to her work. As we might expect, these ingredients lead to an attitude highly ironic. Irony implies detachment and the ability to perceive mean-ing on multiple levels. Flannery O'Connor is acutely aware of such varied possibilities inherent in the life spectacle; and, as author-narrator, she consistently speaks through the voice of the *eiron.* Hence, she is basically unconcerned with prolonged ex-plorations of inner sensibility or with close self-identification with her characters.

Two characters from her work, both minor, strikingly reflect the typical relationship of author and subject. The first is a little old man standing in the line of moviegoers waiting to shake the hand

of Gonga, the gorilla, in *Wise Blood*. When it is the man's turn
to step up, he *skips* forward to greet the celebrity in the hope
that he will call extra attention to himself through his eccentricity.
The author catches forever the old man in his instant of pride;
she records, like a relentless camera, the egoistic caper in the
dance of life.

Just as this character epitomizes mankind exposed in frailty,
a second suggests an image of the author herself, viewing with
impartial severity the human procession passing before her eyes.
This figure appears in *The Violent Bear It Away*, standing in the
doorway of a roadside filling station-grocery, measuring with her
stern gaze the youth returning to his home and to the scene of his
moral failure. At the old man's death, young Tarwater had failed
to complete the burial; he had, in fact, set fire to the house with
the corpse inside in a hysterical rejection of all those values which
his granduncle had attempted to instill in him. The woman in the
doorway, reproaching the negligent boy, "might have had a pair
of wings upon her shoulders." It is thus that Flannery O'Connor
herself views, in large part, the human spectacle. She is like an
austere and—at times—an avenging angel. Revealing man in the
full extent of his egoistic self-blindness, she observes, measures,
and condemns, executing judgment in wild and violent forms of
retribution. Only those survive who transcend or are transformed
by the radical disasters to which they are exposed. She exercises
a stern moral judgment deeply interfused with a sense of the
simultaneously *comic* features of the human scene. When one
looks *with* her, he perceives the comic. When one looks *at* her, he
is suddenly made aware that he—the *hypocrite lecteur*—is himself
being looked at, for the fictional characters but mirror his own
self-image.

It is as yet too early to foresee O'Connor's final position in
American and world letters. Her total output is relatively small,
and her later stories tend toward repetition of earlier themes and
characters. Yet she is undeniably a craftsman of the first rank;
her work exerts a forcefulness of appeal associated with only the
highest talents. Above all, she is characterized by absolute integrity of vision and craft. Indeed, it seems safe to predict that
her work will endure as long as the art of the storyteller is valued
by society—and as long as such things as stories exist.

CHAPTER 2

The Mode: Christian Tragicomedy

IN some respects, O'Connor's basic attitudes run counter to the fashionable intellectual currents of the times. In an age of leniency, she insists upon judgment; in a society of disbelievers, she supports the doctrines of an ancient faith; in a time of alienation, she indicates the paths by which man may recover his lost spiritual heritage. Undoubtedly, such "old-fashioned" views account for much of her attraction, for every age seeks to discover its countenance in its antithetic as well as in its correspondent image. However, to discover more precisely the specific sources of her appeal, we must attend to the *method* which serves the *material*.

Flannery O'Connor is not a technical experimentalist in the conventional sense of the term. She ostensibly utilizes the traditional methods of narrative realism, where easily identifiable characters move through familiar landscapes to encounter experience that is readily comprehensible in its surface aspects. Actions proceed in orderly sequence to evident conclusions; there is no confusing manipulation of point of view, no violent wrenching of chronology, no playful juggling of the interactions between exterior event and interior response. Indeed, she admitted that "So-called experimental fiction always bores me." [1] O'Connor is, however, an innovator in a special sense: she achieves her effects through a fusion of familiar—but highly disparate—elements to attain a "blend" which is peculiarly her own. The reader is asked to respond on many levels simultaneously, and this multileveled approach invests her work with its particular stamp of originality. Flannery O'Connor would have endorsed Blake's view: "Without contraries is no, progression. Attraction and repulsion, reason and energy, love and hate, are necessary to human experience." Her work is charged throughout with the tension bred of contraries—of contradictions of the will set against itself or the world, of the struggle of human effort against divine intention. Ultimately, the many tensions which inform her work on the level of dramatic action are subsumed under, and controlled by, a vision which is at once both tragic and comic, for her world is peopled by characters both laughable and appalling, engaged in actions simultaneously terrifying and absurd.

Her fiction falls into the broad category of tragicomedy, the form now widely recognized as the dominant mode of the age. However, because O'Connor is so deeply preoccupied by religious concerns, the term *Christian tragicomedy* serves especially well to characterize her achievement.[2] And precisely because she is so absorbed in the Christian vision with its deep concern for the redemption of the human spirit through trials of fire and love, her work maintains a striking consistency—of material, pattern, and effect. Her "single story" is the age-old parable of Christian setting forth on his inexorable encounter with the various dragons of this world so that he may proceed toward the heavenly mount. However, her characters must undergo shock, violation, loss to achieve their violent awakenings. Yet—in one sense—their traumas prove to be "heavenly hurts" inflicted upon them so that they may be brought at last to the healing grace of salvation.

However, even her "Christian" vision finds its opposing challenge. Her intention is ever to serve a rigidly Christian view— to present a *meaningful* universe, where human events are enacted within a divinely appointed matrix. Yet, despite her insistence on purpose, grace, and redemption as essential keys in the interpretation of human experience, a contrary implication thrusts itself constantly to the surface of her work. Ultimately, this recurring negative impulse suggests a universe more demonic than angelic, and it arouses speculation as to the possibilities of a nihilistic world order. Out of such contraries spring the electric tensions of her art.

I *The Tension of Contrariety*

Tension of various kinds charges each work of Flannery O'Connor, from the opening statement to the final line. Typically, the tension is introduced in the initial presentation of character. Hazel Motes, for example, is first seen poised tautly on the edge of his train seat, "looking one minute at the window as if he might want to jump out of it, and the next down the aisle at the other end of the car" *(Wise Blood);* Tarwater carouses drunkenly in the creek bed while the corpse of his granduncle, propped at the breakfast table, awaits burial *(The Violent Bear It Away);* and Thomas observes from the upstairs window the arrival of his mother and the "little slut," while rage gathers within him with "ominous intensity, like a mob assembling" ("The Comforts of Home").

Tension may be roused, therefore, by the conflict of inner will against itself (Hazel), by the clash of personal desire with authoritarian structures (Tarwater), or by the bitter opposition of self against others (Thomas). Frequently, the contest is played between the generations: the grandmother quarrels with Bailey Boy and family in "A Good Man Is Hard to Find"; Hulga directs barbed attacks upon the flannel minds of her mother and Mrs. Freeman ("Good Country People"); and various sons chafe under the restrictive ministrations of their doting mothers. Again, the pressures may emerge from the antagonism of race against race ("Everything That Rises Must Converge") or from the resentment of class against class ("Greenleaf").

Ultimately, the various hostilities manifested on the human level derive from man's failure to conform to the dictates of divine intention. Again and again, we encounter the spectacle of pride indulging in willful disregard of obligations of humility, of a covetousness so bound to its commitment to *things* that it is deaf to the call of Christian charity. Pride, covetousness, rage, lust, gluttony, envy, sloth—the full spectrum of a defective humanity is cast before us. God is forgotten, denied, or ignored. However, the holy nexus cannot be so easily broken; the heavenly pursuer overtakes the heedless fugitive at the appropriate juncture. The disparity between divine intention and human act is bridged through dramatic reminders of the abiding covenant.

Such, then, are the initial sources of the tension of her work: the clash of will in conflict with self or other; the antagonisms between levels human and divine, real and ideal, finite and timeless. Even greater tension is achieved, however, by her simultaneous employment of the modes of tragedy and comedy.

II *Christian Tragicomedy*

Among the many dualisms to which O'Connor's work is keyed, the thrust of tragic intention against comic implication is of major importance. Her fiction is weighted with moments of serious illumination issuing from ludicrous circumstance, and undertones of laughter rise in the midst of catastrophe. She herself observed that "Mine is a comic art, but that does not detract from its seriousness." [3] Situation, language, character, action—all reveal a seeming "comic" spirit constantly at work, calling upon us to recognize that the world is peopled by figures essentially laughable in their basic makeup and ludicrous in their typical life response. Our initial reaction may be a superior grin at the spectacle of a world teeming with inanity. But, through our laughter, we are involved; and we are led to reflect upon the most serious questions touching the human experience: the consequences of spiritual violation, the ways by which the aberrant soul is restored to grace. Various devices are employed to convey the seriocomic view: a satiric attitude, abundant grotesquerie, the comic catastrophe, and epiphanies unfolded to unlikely human witnesses.

III *A Satiric View*

Although O'Connor is no *mere* satirist, she employs many of the satirist's characteristic weapons. Foremost among these is the use of the "double view" to expose the pretentions of a folly-ridden universe. The emphasis is ever upon the gap—the ironic discrepancy—between what these figures *claim* for themselves and what they in fact *achieve*. Most frequently, her characters suffer from an excessive vanity, arising from an overweening pride. A recurrent type is the proprietress of the farm, who is inevitably smug in her convictions of inner superiority. Mrs. Cope ("A Circle in the Fire") is convinced that she can handle anything but is helpless in dealing with her delinquent young visitors. Ruby Turpin ("Revelation") thanks the Lord each night for having made her herself instead of some less fortunate creature.

Equally strong in pride are the women helpers on the farm. Mrs. Freeman ("Good Country People") "could never be brought to admit herself wrong on any point." Mrs. Shortley ("The Displaced Person"), threatened by the immigrant Poles, immediately foresees the impending destruction of the entire world except for herself and her own family. Likewise, the mothers must contend with the swollen egos of their intellectual offspring: Joy-Hulga suffers from a bad heart, but "Joy had made it plain that if it had not been for this condition, she would be . . . in a university lecturing to people who knew what she was talking about." And, there are, as well, the many irascible old men who feel they have somehow come into possession of the keys to the universe. For example, Mr. Head ("The Artificial Nigger") is convinced "that age was a choice blessing and that only with years does a man enter into that calm understanding of life that makes him a suitable guide for the young."

Thus, O'Connor sets as one of her foremost aims the puncturing of the swollen self-estimates which her people habitually entertain. The ironic disparity between what the character *is* and what he *assumes* himself to be is emphasized in various ways. Names, for example, often serve ironically to reinforce the flattering self-images of the bearers (as Cope, Hopewell, Head). Other names suggest highly uncomplimentary associations: Mrs. Turpin, whose name is an anagram of turnip; or the two Lucynell Craters ("The Life You Save May Be Your Own"), both conspicuously empty-headed.

Frequently, follies are unmasked when characters engage in situations inherently absurd. Thus Hulga, the wooden-legged lady philosopher, seeks sexual initiation in a hayloft with a backwoods Bible salesman; Enoch, the moronic "apostle" in *Wise Blood*, converts a commode into a gilded shrine and there worships the stolen mummy which he mistakes for the "new jesus"; General Flintrock Poker Sash ("A Late Encounter with the Enemy"), convinced that he is still fetching despite the fact that he is one hundred and eight years old, attends his daughter's graduation ceremony as a treat for the audience and dies onstage.

Again, universal limitations of mind are suggested through the casual inanities which serve for conversation. Mrs. Fox ("The Enduring Chill"), comforting her stricken son, assures him, "People don't die like they used to." The "white-trash woman" in the doctor's office ("Revelation"), after witnessing the bizarre behavior of the Wellesley girl, avers: "I thank Gawd . . . I ain't a lunatic." Virtually every line of dialogue or reported inner reflection serves to satirize the deficient mentality of the commentator. Yet another potent source of satiric reduction is imagery. Mrs. Hitchcock (*Wise Blood*) wearing her hair in "knots" like "dark toad stools"; Julian's mother ("Everything That Rises Must Converge") whose new hat resembles "a cushion with the stuffing out" —these are rendered instantaneously ridiculous through the succinct characterizations. Imagery deflates ego. What the character conveys is not what he intends.

Thus, through revelations of unjustified inner vanity, suggestive names, preposterous situations, banalities of dialogue, and reductive imagery O'Connor emphasizes the alarming discrepancy between inner image and outward impression. These "puffed up" figures provoke our smiles as their follies are laid open before us; but, inwardly, we experience a slight dis-ease as we wonder if our own natures, too, may not be encompassed by certain categories of the inane.

O'Connor has still other satirico-comic weapons at her command. Like Henri Bergson, she stresses the *mechanical* expression of human personality as intrinsically laughable. Typically, her characters display "fixed" qualities in dress, action, and attitude. Caught in the vise of self-hood, they are flat rather than rounded; the stage is frequented by one-sided persons, so wedged in a mold of self that actions seem predetermined, response totally predictable. Clothing, for example, often serves as a summary of personality, a comic reflection of an unchanging inner sense of self. The old lady of "A Good Man Is Hard to Find" dresses as if she were playing the role of "archetypal grandmother":

> the grandmother had on a navy blue straw sailor hat with a bunch of white violets on the brim and a navy blue dress with a small white dot in the print. Her collar and cuffs were white organdy trimmed with lace and at her neckline she had pinned a purple spray of cloth violets containing a sachet. In case of accident, anyone seeing her dead on the highway would know at once that she was a lady.

The grandmother's dress thus reflects a whole range of values deeply associated with the "gentility" with which she so closely identifies herself.

Hazel Motes has consciously rejected his role as a man of God, but his essential identity is betrayed by his "glare-blue" suit and his black preacher's hat. He seeks to camouflage his role as a runaway from God by buying a flashy new hat "exactly the opposite of the old one"; but, after he overhauls it, the new hat is "just as fierce as the old one." Each character wears precisely what he *should* wear. His choice of clothes is determined by the same inner motives which govern his actions, attitudes, and speech.

More significant than details of dress for revealing "automatic" qualities of character are the prevailing attitudes exposed in conversation. Mrs. Cope and Mrs. Pritchard ("A Circle in the Fire") might as well be named Mrs. Optimist and Mrs. Pessimist, for the dialogue between them is a kind of allegorical contest between two opposing points of view. The following exchange is typical:

> "Every day I say a prayer of thanksgiving," Mrs. Cope said. "Think of all we have. Lord," she said and sighed, "we have everything," and she looked around at her rich pastures and hills heavy with timber and shook her head as if it might all be a burden she was trying to shake off her back.
>
> Mrs. Pritchard studied the woods. "All I got is four abscess teeth," she remarked.
>
> "Well, be thankful you don't have five," Mrs. Cope snapped and threw back a clump of grass. "We might all be destroyed by a hurricane. I can always find something to be thankful for."

These two characters are again paired as Mrs. Hopewell and Mrs. Freeman in "Good Country People." Mrs. Hopewell insists that "people who looked on the bright side of things would be beautiful even if they were not." Mrs. Freeman, however, nourishes "a special fondness for the details of secret infections, hidden deformities, assaults upon children." The morning dialogue between these two is an unrelieved exercise in the statement of the obvious:

> "Everybody is different," Mrs. Hopewell said.
> "Yes, most people is," Mrs. Freeman said.
> "It takes all kinds to make the world."
> "I always said it did myself."

Similar banalities pass for conversation in the doctor's office ("Revelation") or on the train *(Wise Blood)*. The speakers rely on clichés instead of ideas, and they construct their "philosophic world-view" from a series of slogans and truisms. In these realistic passages, conversation strangely resembles dialogue from the "theater of the absurd." Not until we are forced to listen closely is the absurdity inherent in everyday experience overwhelmingly exposed.

Most of O'Connor's characters are afflicted with similarly restricted ranges of response. We are in the world of Jonsonian "humours," where the character is so firmly linked to fixed configurations of action and set attitudes that he seems almost to be parodying his own personality. There is little or no refraction of idea before statement, no contemplation of the consequences of action—there is, instead, the stock observation, the habitual gesture. The wire is pulled, the puppet responds to cue. Not until the characters confront some dramatic alteration of circumstance are they forced to an atypical response and thus to emerge as something more than mere comic stereotypes.

O'Connor thus employs her pervasive irony to achieve a highly satiric picture of a folly-ridden world. The spectacle of humanity revealed to us in all its weakness and pride, the constant presentation of figures flattened almost to caricature, awake in us an infinite sense of superiority. At the moment of disaster, however, our satiric targets are suddenly transformed to victims of outrageous calamity, and esthetic distance is abruptly shortened. We then witness a surprise reversal from the essentially comic to the overwhelmingly serious, and we are suddenly sobered by a terrible recognition with the smiles frozen on our faces.

IV *The Grotesque*

The grotesque, a feature which plays such a prominent role in O'Connor's work, also serves to bind the laughable and the serious. O'Connor is obviously intrigued by the radical deviation from the norm, and her work abounds in figures of extreme incongruity. In addition to such obvious examples as the one-legged Hulga and the demented Misfit, we encounter elsewhere in her work hermaphrodites, one-armed carpenters, "blind" preachers, deaf philanthropists, and club-footed child geniuses. Often, bodily imperfection is employed to mirror serious moral deficiency. However, spiritual aberration need not be accompanied by any overt physical symptom. The rapist, the nymphomaniac, the miser—these represent obvious corruptions of spirit.

Because of her heavy insistence upon the physically and morally grotesque, O'Connor's work has frequently been classed as yet another example of "Southern gothic." She herself objected strenuously to the label, for she drew a careful distinction between the terms "gothic" and "grotesque." She insisted that her depictions of grotesque degeneracy served a distinct moral purpose: "Degeneracy . . . at least can be taken in a moral sense. . . . The Gothic is degeneracy which is not recognized as such." [4] Her persistent purpose is to insure that the various degenerates who infest modern society are detected and clearly labeled for what they are. The grotesquerie in O'Connor's work does more, however, than call attention to the moral deviations of the age. It is an important agent in the insertion and ultimate release of esthetic energy within the narratives, for the grotesque vigorously reinforces the tension between comic and tragic modes.

The grotesque, in many of its forms, relies for effect upon a balance between the two contrary impulses of the terrible and the comic. We respond according to the preponderance of emphasis—and thus identify the "horrid" monster, the "funny" clown; but some partial recognition of the contrary motif is always involved. The clown terrifies in the midst of the laughter he provokes, the gargoyle's grin amuses but reminds us also that his suggestive grimace may mask a threat. The spectacle of grotesque deformity also disturbs because it carries with it an implied threat to the established norms of "reality." [5] In its origins, grotesquerie frequently found expression in riotous patterns of flower, animal, imp—images basically drawn from the forms of nature but a nature so transfigured that normal bounds of identity were blurred and threatened to disappear altogether. Even a single grotesque figure reminds us that our familiar world as we experience it is susceptible to violent alteration and that we ourselves are liable to radical transformations of being or even to annihilation. The unexpected departure from the norm is like the Lincoln imp— the surprise variation which raises the question: which, after all, is the ultimate reality—the *Idea* expressed in the basic design or that suggested in the deviation therefrom?

Thus, although we are inclined to laugh at the one-armed carpenter's homely disquisition on the inscrutability of man ("The

Life You Save May Be Your Own"), we, at the same time, are led to speculate about *his* true identity and to ponder the attributes of the evil energy he embodies. The Misfit amuses with his comic investigation of Christian doctrine, but the threat he poses is very real. Likewise, most of O'Connor's grotesques are both amusing and terrifying, for they imply our own potentially destructive involvement with evil, whether we be its victims or its agents. The use of grotesquerie thus maintains a comic-tragic balance; but, at the crucial point, the emphasis shifts abruptly. Amusement is transformed to horror; and, significantly, the reversal occurs so swiftly that we are often still laughing as the victims expire before our startled eyes. The grandmother is funny until she drops in her own blood; Thomas's excessive irritation at the nymphomaniac intruder is amusing until he ends up murdering his mother.

The signals warning of disaster are conveyed most strongly by the obvious deviates: the physically deformed, the spiritually maimed. However, another category of the grotesque in O'Connor's works consists precisely of those types typically classified as "normal." The aberrations of this group generally pass unnoticed by society because they themselves *are* society. They are the everyday, middle-class majority who dominate O'Connor's world; these people, neither flagrant sinners nor striking saints, drift along in the blithe assumption that they represent the "good" aspects of mankind. Their "sins" remain undiscovered by themselves and the world until a major trauma effects exposure, ruin, or salvation. Their initial fault is a lack of faith: "She was a good Christian woman with a large respect for religion, though she did not, of course, believe any of it was true" ("Greenleaf"). Their zealous dedication to *things*—to the operation of a farm, to purchase of machinery, to property and profit—is interpreted by them as evidence of pious Christian industry, not avarice. The nagging grandmothers, the driving widows, the complaining sons —these are "grotesques" if they are set against any ideal pattern. But we are so accustomed to these familiar types that we fail to perceive their deformities until we are forced to observe them at close hand and to listen with full attention.

As O'Connor has observed,

The novelist with Christian concerns will find in modern life distortions which are repugnant to him, and his problem will be to make these appear as distortions to an audience which is used to seeing them as natural; and he may well be forced to take ever more violent means to get his vision across to this hostile audience. When you can assume that your audience holds the same beliefs you do, you can relax a little and use more normal means of talking to it; when you have to assume that it does not, then you have to make your vision apparent by shock—to the hard of hearing you shout, and for the almost blind you draw large and startling figures.[6]

Because the norm is *apathy*, those who are zealous in their spiritual commitments are themselves labeled grotesque by an "uninvolved" society. Old Tarwater and his nephew, Hazel Motes and his waspish grandfather—all appear grotesque in the eyes of an indifferent world. Of her various religious fanatics, O'Connor says: "their fanaticism is a reproach, not simply an eccentricity. Those who, like Amos or Jeremiah, embrace a neglected truth will be seen to be the most grotesque of all." [7] She explains elsewhere: "The prophet-freaks of Southern literature are not images of the man in the street. They are images of the man forced out to meet the extremes of his own nature." [8]

The tragic element of the prophets' natures emerges through the seriousness of their dedication; the *expression* of such commitment is often highly comic. Haze's loss of his car, for example, is the turning point in his final conversion and prepares his return to Jesus; his conversion is a most serious matter. That it arises from the destruction of such a ridiculous object-possession is ludicrous. The prophets are thus figures who become grotesque in the service of good. In her introduction to *Mary Ann*, an account of the life of a child stricken early by an incurable disease, O'Connor observes: "This opened up for me also a new perspective on the grotesque. Most of us have learned to be dispassionate about evil, to look it in the face and find, as often as not, our own grinning reflections with which we do not argue, but good is another matter. Few have stared at that long enough to accept the fact that its face too is grotesque, that in us the good is something under construction." [9]

Thus, O'Connor discovers grotesquerie in all the faces of man—the evil, the apathetic, the good. Her ultimate conclusion is that "we're all grotesque." [10] Our grotesqueness stems from our human status as imperfect reflectors of a divine ideal: "This action by which charity grows invisibly among us, entwining the living and the dead, is called by the Church the Communion of Saints. It is a communion created upon human imperfection, created from what we make of our grotesque state."[11]

V *The Comic Catastrophe*

In Bergson's discussion of the elements of comedy, he notes the "snowball technique" as a familiar comic device; in it, a universe of comic but relatively stable values is gradually threatened and then rapidly overturned in a scene of wild disorder. O'Connor employs a similar "snowball" effect in many of her stories, but in her narrations the issues are so serious and the impetus so great that the snowball seems to carry the action past the point of comedy into the realm of tragedy. The disaster serves as the pivot of the action, swinging the focus swiftly from the comic to the tragic.

"The Artificial Nigger" effectively illustrates O'Connor's use of the "snowball" technique. Mr. Head and his grandson Nelson undergo a series of disturbing but amusing experiences in the city before the wild scene erupts which leads to the startling betrayal of the boy by his grandparent. This crucial scene is carefully paced in a sequence of ever mounting tensions: first, the calm of Nelson sleeping; then the old man's hiding himself in order to play a trick on the boy; Nelson's awakening and tearing wildly down the street, like a panicked animal; the pursuing grandfather discovering the confused scene which results from Nelson's collision with the lady shopper; Nelson's frantically turning to his grandfather for help; and, as the culmination, the patriarch's shocking rejection of his terrified grandson. Thus, the action moves rapidly from the level of foolish deception to serious betrayal—what begins as a game ends in a traumatic disruption of an important human relationship.

Again and again, O'Connor utilizes this "snowball" technique—Julian's mother ("Everything That Rises Must Converge") first annoys the black mother and her child on the bus, then pursues them down the street in a determined attempt to deliver her inappropriate gift, and ends dying on the sidewalk. Thomas in "The Comforts of Home" at first whines absurdly about the intruder in his house, then plots a relatively harmless scheme for getting rid of her, and ends by inadvertently killing his own mother in a violent, surrealist ending.

Thus, although O'Connor seems always to begin in the green world of the pastoral, a world where laughable inanities abound but one where nothing truly calamitous will intrude, we hear, even from the first, echoes of demonic laughter in the distance. Often, our ultimate discovery is that the action is set on the very rim of hell (or heaven, for those who are renewed, rather than ravaged by their experiences). Her actors tread a fragile stage, one ready to break through at any moment, as trap doors are suddenly sprung to catapult the unwary subject to the consuming flames beneath: the family vacation is interrupted by a maniacal assailant; the "innocent" love tryst of Manley and Hulga turns into an obscene assault; children turn from mischief-makers to dangerous arsonists.

Although the *consequence* of catastrophe is extremely serious, the *expression* of it may involve comic implications. The grandmother ("A Good Man Is Hard to Find") in death is a collapsed puppet: she "half sat and half lay in a puddle of blood with her legs crossed under her like a child's and her face smiling up at the cloudless sky." Hazel Motes is a bit ridiculous as he stops off at the outside faucet to wet his newly purchased bucket of lime, in preparation for his sobering act of expiation. O'Connor shows how "comic" events may build to catastrophe, and she likewise exposes the comic residue in disaster.

VI   A Christian Content

If the comment ended when the comic catastrophe produced both laughter and sober reflection, we could assume that we were dealing with another example in the by now familiar genre of essentially "absurd" literature, which views life as a joke played on man. O'Connor, however, does not rest here. She moves out of seeming conventionality into experimentalism—that is, she experiments by superimposing an "orthodox" frame upon unexpected materials. We could dismiss the unfortunate encounter of the grandmother and her family with the homicidal maniac as additional evidence of the chancy nature of human existence if it were not for the "sermon" delivered by the madman in the course of the multiple executions: "Jesus was the only One that ever raised the dead . . . and He shouldn't have done it. He thown everything off balance. If He did what He said, then it's nothing for you to do but thow away everything and follow Him, and if He didn't, then it's nothing for you to do but enjoy the few minutes you got left the best way you can—by killing somebody or burning down his house or doing some other meanness to him. No pleasure but meanness. . . ."

Likewise, the "demonic" children who have come to plague Mrs. Cope laugh from the forest "as if the prophets were dancing in the fiery furnace, in the circle the angel had cleared for them." Mrs. Cope is at last initiated into the mystery of the fall; her face as she moves toward the rising column of smoke "looked as if it might have belonged to anybody; a Negro or a European or to Powell himself."

The insertion of the religious note achieves the transition from the private to the public realm; for religion is, in many of its aspects, a public concern, a common commitment to a set of received ideas. In Flannery O'Connor's view, this set of once universally assumed beliefs has faded dangerously from the modern consciousness. Her intent is to restore its dimmed outlines through severe reminders that man's rejection or ignoring of his traditional spiritual heritage does not diminish its validity nor relieve him of his inner responsibility to fulfill its demands. Through the acid of her art, she etches in vivid outline the nature of that obligation and the consequences of its denial.

Because of the deep religious convictions in which her work is grounded, the fiction of Flannery O'Connor displays a remarkable unity of purpose and consistency of theme. Her abiding concern— the ever-present daemon which haunts her pages at every turn— is the desperate need of man to open himself to the visitation of the Holy Spirit: to let his dead conscience be stirred to life and so reestablish the bond by which flesh is recognized as but the sanctuary of the sacred energy. Thus, because she perceives grace as the central need of human experience and redemption as the essential aim of life itself, she also insists on the reality of sin and the inevitability of judgment. Unlike many modernists who complain that God has turned His back on the world, she contends that it is man who now shuns God. She holds no sympathy for relativistic ethical codes, and she brooks no tolerance for humanistic credos which in her view have led mankind disastrously far

from the divine center. Much of what modern man terms "progress" she dismisses as the result of faulty judgment on the part
of those blinded by the fumes of hell. Foremost among the devil's
tricks is his clever insistence that he himself no longer exists, and
thus sin, judgment, and redemption are archaisms lacking ap-
plicability to modern experience. "Adjustment," "progress," "enlightenment"—these are anathema in her view.

Though O'Connor protests that she is "congenitally innocent
of doctrine," her works rest on a clearly discernible doctrinal
base. Starting from a recognition of the fall and its corollary notion of original sin, she proceeds through conventional—but today widely ignored—categories of atonement, grace, salvation.
Though she is frequently considered a pessimist by those who
resent her heavy emphasis on the ugliness inherent in the spectacle of a world gone awry, she is, in fact, ultimately optimistic
in that she clearly envisions salvation—with its cognate promise
of eternal life—as potentially attainable by the human soul. The
path to the cross is, however, never easy; the journey is a movement marked by violence, suffering, often acute disaster. To
arouse the recipients of grace, divinity often resorts to drastic
modes of awakening. The two novels and the nineteen stories
collected during O'Connor's lifetime offer a full exploration of the
diverse methods—direct and indirect—by which the soul may be
recalled to redemption or, in other instances, brought to judgment.

The prophets of the two novels—Hazel Motes and Mason Tarwater—are haunted by the divine specter until they humbly ac-
cede and conform their purposes to its own. Haze stares too long
at the follies of mankind; at last he finds the light of truth in a
world of darkness; Tarwater—the fiery evangelist—gags upon
human food until he admits that his hunger can be assuaged only
by the bread of life. In similar fashion, Obadiah Elihu Parker
("Parker's Back") and Asbury Fox ("The Enduring Chill") are
driven to grace, for each is the startled recipient of a supernatural
sign of election.

Others, more stolidly wedged in apathy, must be exposed to
even more violent awakenings; they are threatened, assaulted, or
even annihilated as the price of regeneration. Here, O'Connor relies on a highly paradoxical view of salvation: redemption through
catastrophe. To this category belong Mrs. Cope of "A Circle in the

Fire," whose cherished "property" must be destroyed so that her lack of charity may be exposed; the arrogant Hulga ("Good Country People"), whose foolish denial of evil is dramatically refuted by the ignorant backwoods impostor; Mrs. Turpin ("Revelation"), who is first insulted, then assaulted, by the unlovely Wellesley girl in preparation for her illumination; Mrs. May, of "Greenleaf," who comes at last to understanding of the operation of mercy as she is being impaled on the horns of a maddened bull; and the foolish grandmother ("A Good Man Is Hard to Find"), shot down by a maniac in cold blood, but not before she experiences that influx of love which is the mark of her final election. Fire, rapes physical and spiritual, homicide—all are weapons of the divine arsenal.

In addition to those stories which present grace or illumination as a consequence of violence inflicted upon the divinely appointed victim, another group ultilizes the reverse pattern: the recipient of "election" himself becomes the victimizer. The result of his betrayal is his entrance upon the course of guilt and suffering which will bring him to redemption or, if he fails to heed their lessons, seal his damnation. Thus Mr. Head ("The Artificial Nigger") discovers the extent of his own insufficiency in his cowardly denial of his grandson before the world; Mrs. McIntyre ("The Displaced Person") is left to contemplate in her prolonged debility the horror of her failure to prevent the death of the hapless Pole; children—through failure of compassion and understanding—unwittingly prepare the deaths of their parents (Julian in "Everything That Rises Must Converge" and Tanner's daughter in "Judgement Day"); likewise, callous parents drive their offspring to seek in death an alleviation of the vacuity of existence ("The Lame Shall Enter First" and "The River").

The immediate consequences of such various betrayals—through denial, the failure of sympathy, the withholding of love—are serious enough in themselves. And O'Connor does not spare the offenders the harshest of judgments. They are totally culpable for their "sins of omission" and are left to expiate fully through suffering and awareness of guilt the burden of their misdeeds. Yet—and here is the second paradox in her view of the unpredictable methods of the Holy Redeemer—the guilty, suffering spirit is a more likely recipient of grace than the apathetic soul smugly entrenched in notions of its own moral superiority. Thus violence

—committed upon the human candidate or indirectly fostered (upon others) through failure to act—plays a major role in O'Connor's works as a drastic means of redemption.

The acts of violence in the second volume of stories are in some respects more shocking than those in the first, for over half the stories in *Everything That Rises Must Converge* deal with the fatal betrayal of parent (or surrogate) by child, or vice versa. Two of these tales are particularly chilling, for in them the disaster is effected through the *direct* act of violence by the human agent against his most beloved blood relation. Thomas ("The Comforts of Home") inadvertently slays his mother when he aims at the wanton intruder. In "A View of the Woods," however, we witness what is possibly the most macabre scene in all O'Connor's works—the spectacle of an enraged septuagenarian literally beating his nine-year-old granddaughter to death when she offends his own inflated notion of pride. In this story alone, no hope of salvation is extended. The instruction is, rather, in the consequence of indulgence in at least three of the seven deadly sins—wrath bred of pride and covetousness.

Thus O'Connor characteristically links salvation to the act of violence—and the candidate for redemption may fall into the role of either victim or victimizer. The operations of the divine spiritual agency are frequently contrary to human notions of reason or justice. For the whole is ever shrouded in mystery, which the human observer may witness or participate in—but never fully comprehend:

> The serious fiction writer will think that any story that can be entirely explained by the adequate motivation of the characters or by a believable imitation of a way of life or by a proper theology, will not be a large enough story for him to occupy himself with. This is not to say that he doesn't have to be concerned with adequate motivation or accurate reference or a right theology; he does; but he has to be concerned with them only because the meaning of his story does not begin except at a depth where these things have been exhausted. The fiction writer presents mystery through manners, grace through nature, but when he finishes, there always has to be left over that sense of Mystery which cannot be accounted for by any human formula.[12]

A final category of O'Connor's work seeks to explore the mystery that pervades all aspects of human experience. These stories— five in number—all appear in *A Good Man Is Hard to Find*, and all either pertain to the mystery inherent in the sacraments themselves or reflect a strongly sacramental view of life. "The River" presents the startling testimony of a baptism which becomes a literal dying into life; "A Temple of the Holy Ghost" dwells upon the recurrent enigma of the spirit made flesh, as attested in the paradox of the Eucharist ceremony; and "The Life You Save May Be Your Own" examines the spectacle of an evil which views matrimony not as a divinely sanctioned union but as an opportunity to realize its own selfish aims. Failures to perceive the sacramental nature of birth and death are depicted in "A Stroke of Good Fortune" and "A Late Encounter with the Enemy."

In her addition of the religious dimension to her comic-disastrous structure, Flannery O'Connor arrives at what may justly be described as an original creation. As we have noted, tragicomedy as such is the predominant mode of the age,[13] and O'Connor relies on the mixture of form favored by her contemporaries; but she reverses the usual categories of interpretation. In her view, man is absurd not because his inherent nature is to be ludicrous but because he deliberately shuns God. His suffering is not an unmerited and inexplicable sentence inflicted by a congeries of unspecified social and genetic determinants; it is justifiable chastisement for "sin" or it is a spiritual agony undertaken to attain traditional patterns of redemption. Nothing in the message is essentially new, for it repeats the content of Christian sermonizing of many centuries. It is, however, a rare utterance for an artist of this century. And the forms in which the message is decked make it unique: it issues as a *Christian tragicomedy* where disaster is meaningful and man can still claim—or reject—his ancient spiritual heritage as the child of God.

VII   *A Demonic Thrust*

Flannery O'Connor's effects are achieved, therefore, through the manipulation of satiric, grotesque, and catastrophic elements to produce a special brand of tragicomedy. The initial emphasis is on the comic response, but undertones of disaster are present from

the first; and, in the inevitable reversal, tragedy outweighs comedy. The intention is to achieve a resolution—an explanation of
the meaning of catastrophe—through established categories of
religious interpretation. The emphasis is on a positive view of
man's ultimate fate: since heaven and hell exist as realities, man
can, by correcting his erroneous ways, avoid the latter and attain
the former.

Yet, admittedly, some doubts remain in the consciousness of the
uncommitted reader, who can argue that O'Connor's terms do
not, finally, apply; that everything has not, in fact, been adequately accounted for. John Hawkes, in particular, accuses O'Connor of using "the devil's voice as a vehicle for satire." In his view,
"the creative process transforms the writer's objective Catholic
knowledge of the devil into an authorial attitude in itself some
measure diabolic." [14] Although O'Connor denied his accusation,
as did Brainard Cheney in a heated refutation,[15] Hawkes's con-
tention is intriguing, especially if we accept Baudelaire's premise
that to laugh at the deficiencies of another is an act of pride;
hence, laughter itself is the devil's creation. Flannery O'Connor
consistently calls upon her reader to share with her an implicitly
superior view of her self-limited subjects. Only at the moment
of cataclysm—when we watch in horror as the "victims" are demol-
ished or discover their participation in the unintended destruction
of others—is our laughter silenced; and then we uneasily begin
to suspect that we have been overly hasty in our judgments.

Furthermore, O'Connor's insistence upon catastrophe as the
omnipresent factor in human experience urges the "demonic"
vision, a sense of existence constantly assailed by dark forces
working against man's welfare, ready to spring forth at the un-
guarded moment to threaten or cancel life itself in bizarre circumstances of defeat. Finally, though the religious postulates implicit
in the narrations point toward affirmative avowals, the events
themselves are open to quite dissimilar interpretations. Is the
grandmother a recipient of grace or a victim of malign madness?
Is Bevel ("The River") saved by truth or destroyed through a
pitiable commitment to illusion? Is the hermaphrodite proof of
"mystery" or testimony to a malevolent or indifferent creation?

Thus, some element of unallayed tension, of unresolved dilemma, remains to the end. This pervasive ambivalence—the contrary pulls toward "affirmation" and "negation"—accounts, I think,

for much of the misunderstanding which O'Connor's early work aroused and for the continuing bafflement of many first-time readers. It suggests why such highly contradictory interpretations of her meaning continue to appear in the critical journals, but it also explains, I believe, the insistent appeal of her work for an age which would like to believe but has—for the most part—lost the instruments of faith.

A mocking attitude toward humanity, universal cataclysm, conclusions which carry threatening implications—these suggest that the world is prey to forces less than benevolent. Flannery O'Connor's vision as articulated in her own commentaries *about* her work and *about* the role of the artist make clear that she intends to fulfill the "prophetic" role through her writing: she would instruct the world in the proper paths to redemption through the clarity of her vision. But the contrary implications aroused by her works are not thereby fully answered.

O'Connor's overall forcefulness as a writer thus develops from a series of ever increasing tensions: conflicts on the level of character and action; opposition achieved by setting the techniques of comedy against those of tragedy; and, most significant, a consciously Christian vision at war with an alternative (though unconscious) "demonic" view.

CHAPTER *3*

Pattern of Salvation: *Wise Blood*

WHEN the novel *Wise Blood* was published in 1952, it met with a variety of response that ranged from baffled incomprehension to sincere applause. The reviewer in *Newsweek*, while admitting that "Flannery O'Connor is perhaps the most gifted of the youngest generation of American novelists," skirted the problem of interpreting its meaning, concluding lamely that "readers can make of Haze's legend what they will." [1] *Time Magazine,* which went a step further, explained that the book traced the experience of a "red-necked fanatic" who "deliberately blinds himself because a mean-spirited cop has pushed his unlicensed Essex over a cliff." [2] To Isaac Rosenfeld, Motes was "plain crazy," and hence no one could "take his predicament seriously." [3]

It was perhaps understandable that the early readers of O'Connor were confused. For, like all first-rate artists, she dared to confront her audience with startling and original effects. Certain of her materials were drawn from the realm of the familiar— the details of the stark Georgia landscape, the country types easily identifiable as descendants of the early frontier, and grotesques similar to those that have peopled Southern literature for so many years. But she added to these familiar elements a final feature which mystified and disturbed. For, as we have observed, O'Connor is, above all, a Christian writer; and her bizarre narratives of absurdly comic Southerners are governed by the stern purity of a rigidly Christian view.

Hazel Motes of *Wise Blood* is essentially a tragic figure in a comic universe, and the work in which he appears is thus a special form of tragicomedy. The world of Taulkingham is peopled by grotesques who are ludicrous because they have rejected the possibility of grace. Haze's tragedy arises out of his predicament as a man committed to belief (or nonbelief, in certain stages of his life) who is condemned to move through an uncommitted world:

"Jesus been dead a long time" and nobody really cares. Even when Haze is deliberately pursuing anti-Christ, he is saved from total absorption into the triviality of his surroundings. In addition to his ultraserious dedication to the task at hand (denying Christ and setting up the new "Church Without Christ"), there is ever present in the reader's mind the recollection of Haze's grandfather and of Haze's rejected vocation of preacher. These hover always over the present action, placing Haze in perspective as one who is a (temporarily) "lost soul" by virtue of the fact that he *has a soul* to lose.

Thus, the tension between his former Christian dedication and his present deviation serves to balance Haze's outward absurdities —his ridiculous wardrobe, his social ineptness in the dining car, his difficulties as a driver—with a weight of meaning that prevents him from ever becoming *merely* a comic figure. The *content* of his experience—sin, atonement, redemption—is totally serious; but the *expression* of it frequently verges on the ludicrous. At the end, we see him restored to the world of tragedy; but even then he retains in character and situation some traces of the comic universe which surrounds and earlier threatened to overwhelm him.

Many writers have, of course, experimented with the fusion of comic and serious elements in a single work. The black humorists, the practitioners of the "theater of the absurd," the makers of such films as *Bonnie and Clyde* and *Dr. Strangelove*—all confront us with a radical fusion of hilarity and despair. In fact, Thomas Mann observes: "For I feel that, broadly and essentially, the achievement of modern art is that it has ceased to recognize the categories of tragic and comic or the dramatic classifications, tragedy and comedy, and views life as tragicomedy." [4]

Flannery O'Connor deals with extremes. In *Wise Blood,* she creates a modern saint's legend within a comic setting. The work is a study of conversion in both a religious and artistic sense. Hazel Motes, the comically pathetic runaway from God, is at last trapped by his destiny; and the story is thereby transformed from a seeming exercise in farce to a most intently serious study of the problem of redemption in the modern world.

I   A Runaway from God

The action of *Wise Blood* develops through a basic pattern of flight, apprehension, and capitulation. The fugitive is Hazel

Motes, seeking, like Jonah, to escape his divinely appointed mission. Haze had planned to become a preacher; but, having lost his faith while in the army, he dedicates his life to anti-Christ instead. In his search for the "new jesus," he plunges into the secular city, and there he encounters various alternatives to (but also, in effect, embodiments of) his projected "Church Without Christ." Sex, idolatry, commercialized religion, and ritualized commerce—all provide potential modes of confirming his role as the devil's disciple. In the end, however, Haze is unable to maintain his status as Satan's emissary. He deserts Sabbath Lily, smashes the mummy-gift of Enoch against the wall, and runs over his own preacher-twin. However, he himself is assaulted on the way out of town: when the lawman sends Haze's ancient auto crashing over the cliff, Haze recognizes that God has at last given him a "sign." Without hesitation, he returns to town and blinds himself as a drastic act of atonement for his futile efforts to flee from grace.

Haze, as he is first presented on the train to Taulkingham, is slightly ridiculous in his glare-blue suit with the price tag still on it and his wide-brimmed black preacher's hat, which is pulled fiercely down on his brow. Haze is clearly a man with a mission: his face proclaims his destiny, for it is the visage of a saint. The outline of the skull, plain and insistent beneath the flesh, the nose fierce like a shrike's bill, the deep creases on either side of the mouth—these details might well characterize the Saint Jerome of El Greco or the face of an old-world prophet in the Sistine Chapel. But most arresting are his eyes, set deep within their hollow sockets; and indeed images of sight and seeing—employed in the ancient equation of inner vision with knowledge—provide the unifying metaphor of the work. Each iteration of sight imagery is resonant with biblical echoes: "Now we see as through a glass darkly . . . If thy right eye offend thee . . . An eye for an eye . . ." and, above all, "They have eyes and see not." When we first encounter Haze, he is engaged in a typical action—he is looking intently at something which his companion cannot discern. His first spoken words in the narrative are, "I got to go *see* the porter."

The eyes of Hazel Motes—"like passages leading somewhere"—are the central feature of his countenance, the visible sign of his inward identity. The name itself specifies this essential trait of the man, for *Hazel* suggests the hue of his eyes ("the color of pecan shells") and *Motes* recalls to us the biblical injunction, "first cast out the beam out of thine own eye; and then thou shalt see clearly to cast out the *mote* out of thy brother's eye." This casting out the beam is, of course, precisely what Hazel does in a most literal fashion when he, like Oedipus, serves as priest and penitent, divine executioner and human victim, exacting fierce retribution for the guilt of an unholy life.[5] The dramatic force of the gesture is prepared for through constant references to sight and sightlessness—the glasses of his mother which Hazel carries with him as a reminder of home, the phony preacher who trades upon his feigned blindness in his evangelistic con game, the bastard child-strumpet who gives Haze "the eye," the shining eye of the owl gazing accusingly at Haze out of the darkness of his cage in the city zoo. Flannery O'Connor, like Sophocles, uses the physical act of blinding not merely for its dramatic impact but also to awaken the full force of the many symbolic implications of sight-ignorance, blindness-knowledge, light-darkness, death-life.

His name, then, captures the essence of the man as the seeing unbeliever who becomes the blinded seer. Most often, the first name is shortened to simply *Haze*, suggesting mist or cloud; and this abbreviation in turn defines the moral state of Hazel throughout the early course of the action. In fact, when we first see him, he is a victim of a divided intention: "looking one minute at the window as if he might want to jump out of it, and the next down the aisle at the other end of the car." Haze is at this stage in a very real sense a "divided self."

Haze is the grandson of a country preacher, "a waspish old man who had ridden over three counties with Jesus hidden in his head like a stinger." The backwoods prophet had arrived in Eastrod, Tennessee, every fourth Saturday "as if he were just in time to save them all from Hell, and he was shouting before he had the car door open." Hazel had known by the time he was twelve that he too would follow the preacher's calling: "he saw Jesus move from tree to tree in the back of his mind, a wild ragged figure motioning him to turn around and come off into the dark." At eighteen, when the army called him, he sensed at once the "trick to lead him into temptation"; but he was confident of his ability to return home uncorrupted in a few months. When he is released, four years later, Eastrod is no longer there, and Hazel has been "converted to nothing instead of to evil." He is on his way to the city of Taulkingham to preach the new gospel of the "Church Without Christ." His appearance and manner are still very much those of the fundamentalist disciple, and he is often taken for one. In town, the taxi driver sizes him up at once for a preacher:

"You look like a preacher," the driver said. "That hat looks like a preacher's hat."
"It ain't," Haze said, and leaned forward and gripped the back of the front seat. "It's just a hat."

The blind preacher senses at once that "Some preacher has left his mark on you." Even Enoch, Haze's unsought companion, taunts him: "I knew when I first seen you you didn't have nobody nor nothing but Jesus."

Hazel is also divided against the world, and the early indications of this conflict are seen in the opening episode, specifically through his attempts to communicate with those who ignore or insult him and through his own rejection of those who try to engage his attention or his interest. When Haze does initiate conversation, it is on the most direct and meaningful level. For example, he accosts the porter with the assertion that the black man is in fact a "Parrum nigger from Eastrod," but the porter insists that he is from Chicago. This encounter is one of Haze's many attempts to define things for what they are, and the porter's denial of his identity is the first of many instances in the story of Haze confronting those who reject their selfhood, assuming instead various disguises. To Mrs. Hitchcock, Haze delivers his scornful taunt: "I reckon you think you been redeemed." Obviously taken aback, she counters with the empty observation that life is an inspiration. In the dining car, he confides to the ladies with the red-speared nails that he does not believe in Jesus, would not if He were on the train, to which confession he receives the scornful retort, "Who said you had to?"

In these various reactions, Haze encounters the responses which are to characterize the attitudes of the city dwellers—denial of truth (the porter), embarrassed refusal to approach the subject seriously (Mrs. Hitchcock), and contemptuous rejection (ladies in the diner); and in these mutually futile attempts at communication is conveyed the second major strand of imagery, images of sound ("Though ye have ears ye hear not . . .").

Haze is thus a man obviously at war with himself and society. He assumes that, since Jesus is a fraud, the way to deny him most effectively is through a life of deliberate sin. He chooses the two most direct routes to the devil—sexual impurity and open blasphemy. At Mrs. Watts's residence he is initiated into sex (not too successfully), and on the street he begins his formal preachment of the tenets of his new church—the Church Without Christ. Standing on the nose of his car (like his grandfather before him), he shouts:

> . . . I preach the Church Without Christ. I'm member and preacher to that church where the blind don't see and the lame don't walk and what's dead stays that way. Ask me about that church and I'll tell you it's the church that the blood of Jesus don't foul with redemption.
>
> • • •
>
> . . . I'm going to preach there was no Fall because there was nothing to fall from and no Redemption because there was no Fall and no Judgment because there wasn't the first two. Nothing matters but that Jesus was a liar.

Later on, he issues his call for the "new jesus": ". . . The Church Without Christ don't have a Jesus but it needs one! It needs a new jesus! It needs one that's all man, without blood to waste, and it needs one that don't look like any other man so you'll look at him. Give me such a jesus, you people. Give me such a new jesus and you'll see how far the Church Without Christ can go!"

II   *The New Jesus and the Secular City*

The city, of course, has long since discovered for itself various embodiments of the "new jesus," with appropriate rituals, tabernacles, and presiding deities. Mrs. Watts, a sex goddess whose adherents advertize her virtues in a public convenience, is discovered enshrined in a rumpled bed. For the worshipers of gadgets, the potato-peeler salesman displays his relics from his sidewalk "altar," intoning the merits of his wares in a familiar modern liturgy. The operator of Slade's Used Car Lot faithfully follows the accustomed ritual of sale and purchase, solemnly affirming the mystical benefits that will accrue to owner of the sacred sale item. Some, however, still employ the outworn forms of an antique faith to purvey their wares. Asa Hawks does just what his name implies—he hawks his religious merchandise in the streets, offering the compromise of silence for those who would "rather have him beg than preach."

Enoch of the "wise blood" finds a still more primitive deity— the shrunken mummy for which he prepares a splendid tabernacle in the form of a gilded commode. Having worshiped in an appropriate ceremony, he delivers the holy idol to the unappreciative Haze. His role as divine agent accomplished, Enoch goes lusting after a still stranger god: Gonga, the presiding deity of the modern movie set. Enoch is rewarded for his adulation, for he ultimately becomes the god; he exchanges his own clothes and familiar identity for the costume and mystical selfhood of Gonga.

In the street, Haze encounters yet other would-be messiahs of the present age. He early acquires an unwanted disciple, Hoover Shoates, who "looked like a preacher turned cowboy or a cowboy turned mortician." The street philosophy expounded by Hoover Shoates—and later, by his disciple Solace Layfield—embodies the extremes of ethical relativism. Significantly, Hoover labels his mission the "Holy Church of Christ Without Christ." The change from Haze's simple "Church Without Christ" is meaningful; it is quite possible to have a church without Christ, but it is hardly possible to have a "Church of Christ Without Christ." In this name for Hoover's church is revealed, however, the peculiar paradox of the modern city, many of whose inhabitants embrace a nominal Christianity but reject all the tenets of traditional Christian doctrine. Hoover (or Onnie Jay Holy, as he calls himself for professional purposes) offers Christ without tears and salvation without suffering in a peculiar "do-it-yourself" religious formula: "The unredeemed are redeeming themselves and the new jesus is at hand! Watch for the miracle! Help yourself to salvation in the Holy Church of Christ Without Christ."

According to Hoover, the notion of original sin is passé, for the true believer knows that "Every person that comes onto this earth . . . is born sweet and full of love." All mystery is dispelled: "You don't have to believe nothing you don't understand and approve of. If you don't understand it, it ain't true, and that's all there is to it. . . . You can sit at home and interpit your own Bible

however you feel in your heart it ought to be interpited . . . just
the way Jesus would have done it." Salvation, like love and
potato peelers, is available for a small cash outlay: "It'll cost you
each a dollar, but what is a dollar? A few dimes! Not too much
to pay to unlock that little rose of sweetness inside you!"

Recognizing a phony, Haze rebuffs Hoover's invitation to form
a partnership, and he ends their relationship by throwing Hoover
out of his car and slamming the door on his hand. But Haze, like
Gonga, soon discovers that it is not always safe to reject a would-
be disciple. As Hoover had threatened, he shows up as an aggressive competitor, equipped with his own convert who is a second
Haze—car, suit, and all. In astonished frustration, Haze observes
his avowed beliefs presented in a grotesque inversion by the in-
terlopers. Haze soon leaves in disgust, but the crowd is obviously
interested.

A final avatar of the new jesus is suggested by the lady who
offers advice to the troubled in her newspaper column. When
Sabbath Lily, disturbed by the fact that as a bastard she is automatically barred from heaven, wonders if she should "neck,"
Mary Brittle counsels, "your real problem is one of adjustment to
the modern world . . . a religious experience can be a beautiful
addition to living if you put it in the proper perspective and do
not let it warp you. Read some books on Ethical Culture."

These, then, are the cults of the secular world—sex, things,
glamour, adjustment, and various perversions of the religious
sentiment, ancient and modern. The new paganism produces not
harmony but disharmony at all levels. Man is at war with all
categories—animal, human, divine. The novel is charged with the
tension of conflicting motives, constant efforts at fraud and exploitation; the words of the blessing are transformed into a curse,
repeated so often their sacred connotations are forgotten.

Tension is sustained in the novel from the opening scene
through the final pages. The action begins with Haze poised
tensely upon the edge of his seat, ready for action. The tension is
reinforced by the various futile attempts at communication, both
on the train and in the city. Insults are freely traded by the
residents of the secular city. The cop crudely chastises Hazel for
failing to observe the light signal: "Maybe you thought the red
ones was for white folks and the green ones for niggers." When
Haze stops the Essex on the highway to read a sign, the truck

driver asks, "Will you get your goddam outhouse off the middle
of the road?" The cop who performs the last rites on the Essex
sneers: "I just don't like your face."

The sense of psychological tension is extended to the realm of
physical action. When Enoch refuses to reveal the preacher's
address, Haze flings a rock, knocking Enoch unconscious. Haze
kicks the false disciple out of his car, slamming Hoover's hand
in the door in the process. Haze demolishes the "new jesus"
proffered by Enoch in a frenzy of destruction, completing the
"murder" by flinging the mummy's empty skin out the back door
to the garbage area below. Haze runs over the fleeing "preacher
twin" not once, but twice, terminating his last-gasp confessional
with a robust slap on the back. And Haze himself becomes the
victim of aggression when the patrolman brutally shoves his car
over the embankment and when the town cops finish him off
with a tap on the head as he lies dying in a drainage ditch.

Even inanimate objects partake of the universal antagonism.
When Haze sleeps alone at the deserted homestead, a board falls
on his head in the night. Enoch goes into a frenzy attempting to
operate the unruly umbrella with its menacing dog's head handle.
When Enoch labors to beautify the decaying chair in his room,
he is not sure "whether it was for him or against him." These
various hostilities—man against man, man against things—are, of
course, reflections of the greater rift between human and divine.
A snarling, sullen, sour world—this is what man produces when
he builds from an unholy foundation.

III   *The Creature More than the Creator*

To reflect the disparity that exists between the unrealized
divine potential and the gross actuality, O'Connor uses familiar
images of the animal kingdom. These images culminate in the
curious action of Enoch Emery, who, in order to establish his
rightful position in the universe, rejects the human role entirely
and becomes—in appearance at least—the beast incarnate.
Throughout the novel, animals help to establish the literal landscape: the hogs like stones seen by Haze out the train window;
the cow, ambling away; and the buzzard, circling into the distance as the car is sent crashing over the bluff by the aggressive
patrolman. Frequently, however, animal imagery is attached to

the human figure, either through figurative language or by a sur-
name; and thus it serves the obvious function of reductive characterization (Asa Hawks, Hoover Shoates). Often, the animal
image is used to achieve a swift insight into character: Haze's
nose is "like a shrike's bill"; Hawks laughs like a "grinning man-
dril"; Enoch himself resembles a "friendly hound dog with light
mange." Frequently, a detail of dress or appearance emphasizes
the essential absurdity of character: the ladies "dressed like parrots" or the potato peeler salesman's shirt "patterned with
bunches of upside-down pheasants and quail and bronze turkeys."
Often categories are confused and the animal level intrudes upon
the human (the cow dressed like a housewife), or the human
descends below the animal level to the inanimate (the lady wearing a rubber tire in the advertisement). These various images
underline man's failure to realize his identity, capture his role,
or find his true place in the secular city.

All these animal images culminate in the character of Enoch
Emery, who, with his "wise blood," is more acutely conscious of
the animal realm, sensing both its menace and its attractions.[6]
Enoch is early associated with the animal level by his occupation
—he is a guard at the zoo. He feels that here—in the park—he is
in the heart of the city and that he has demonstrated his own
perceptiveness by going at once to this center. Enoch, who is
intensely conscious of his own relationship to the animal world,
visits the animals in a daily ritual, hurling practiced obscenities
at the indifferent subjects. He envies their easy existence (they
have no work to do, and are fed T-bone steaks daily by the
attendants). At the same time, his envy is mixed with fear. He
senses a definite menace from the animal realm, particularly from
the moose gazing forbodingly from the wall in his room. When
he embarks on his mysterious project, his first action is to render
the moose impotent by deframing it, the equivalent of undressing
it. He knows something significant is about to happen, and he
does not want the moose to run things.

Gonga, the gorilla, is for Enoch the epitome of success. Gonga
does, in fact, possess all the attributes essential to success in the
modern age—power, celebrity, personal magnetism. As Enoch
approaches for the magic handshake, he prepares a mental insult;
but, at the moment of contact, his will fails, and he blurts out a
confession of identity. Such snarling rejection by his idol leads

Enoch to execute a singular vengeance. He attacks Gonga and dresses himself in the beastly garb. Once in the gorilla suit, Enoch feels himself endowed with peculiar physical and personal powers that will ensure his future success. Enoch's overt fusion with a lower order—his attempted transformation of his human role into a bestial one—is merely an effort on his part to achieve in a literal sense what modern society metaphorically enacts daily in its typical speech, dress, and attitudes. When Sabbath Lily welcomes Haze to bed, she calls him "King of the Beasts," apparently the highest compliment she can bestow. The all-pervasive references to the animal kingdom suggest that man must either transcend the human level or fall back to some earlier stage in the evolutionary processes. Having failed as human, Enoch opts for the beast. Enoch vanishes from the novel at the point of his downward transformation. His abrupt disappearance has been called a flaw in the novel, but one of his biblical namesakes, Enoch of the seventh generation from Adam, also was taken mysteriously from the sight of man, being transported by deity. Likewise, Enoch Emery's god seems at last to have rewarded him.

Enoch, whose life is governed by deep intuitions, is particularly attuned to supernatural signs and tokens. Indeed, signs function as a major motif within the novel. There are, first, the signs which label the data of experience—

FROSTY BOTTLE
SLADE'S FOR THE LATEST
GONGA!
Giant Jungle Monarch and a Great Star!

There are, second, the signs of the road that call the errant sinner to repentance—"Jesus Died for you." These religious slogans, along with the curses which echo constantly in the background, serve as recurrent reminders of the religious frame of the work. Haze as a boy waited in vain for a "sign" in the woods; later, in the patrolman's destruction of his car, Haze detects the unmistakable hand of God. It is the sign he has waited for, for so long, the event which dramatically reverses the course of his life.

Enoch is convinced that it is his blood which tells him what to do—the wise blood that he inherited from his daddy. Blood itself forms another major symbolic motif in the novel. Literally, blood is shed at various points in the narrative, as when Haze heaves a rock at Enoch's head and when the barbed wire cuts the flesh of Haze's chest. Again, blood operates as a connection between the physiological and emotional levels of response which are revealed when faces flush or whiten from anger or vexation. Owen Barfield in his *Saving the Appearances* notes the degree to which modern man, despite his sophistication in many respects, still participates in the elemental blood response to external stimuli:

> The word *blood* is a particularly striking example of such a shift of meaning, since it is a substance with which, as it swings to and fro from heart and lung at the centre to visible complexion and sensitive skin at the periphery, we can still in some measure feel ourselves to be united by an extra-sensory link. We can, for example, both feel within ourselves and see through the curtain of another's flesh how instantly it answers to fear and shame. Thus, we still participate "originally" in our own blood up to the very moment when it becomes phenomenal by being shed. From that moment on, we abandon it to the mechanomorphism which characterizes all our phenomena. For us—that is, for our casual awareness, though not for our scientific concepts—there are really two kinds of blood: the shed and the unshed; rather as for Galen there were two kinds of blood, the venous and the arterial. Both of Galen's were participated; whereas only *one* of ours is. We refer to what remains of that participation when we speak, with a psychological intention, of "bad blood" or "hot blood." We no longer distinguish where he did. We do distinguish where he did not, polarizing the old meaning of *blood* into two, a metaphorical and a literal one. And our medicine interests itself almost exclusively in the literal one, that is, in the idol.[7]

Thus, blood may be regarded as phenomenon; or as a link between man's physical and emotional reactions; or—as with Enoch's view—it may be considered as a source of the mysterious "divine" promptings which take precedence over all demands of logic or rationality. Blood as a symbolic element in *Wise Blood* takes on its highest meaning as a reference to the sacrifice on the cross and to the subsequent redemption of man. It is, finally, not Enoch but Haze who is possessed of "wise blood"; and the Christ-pattern he follows is unmistakable. Just as Haze's total personality is set in vivid contrast to Enoch's absurdity, so the implicit allusions to

the blood of the cross and to the profound sacrifice there enacted
serve as an ironic reminder of the essential triviality of Enoch's
pursuits. O'Connor herself referred to Enoch as "a moron and
chiefly a comic character." [8] In his wild pursuit of mystic truth,
he anticipates such later fanatics as Mrs. Shortley ("The Displaced
Person") who prophesies universal disaster, and Mrs. Greenleaf
("Greenleaf") who practices "prayer healing." These characters
reflect, in their various ways, the primitive urge toward idolatry
which survives even amidst the intellectual sophistications of the
present age.

In fact, Enoch epitomizes the spirit of the secular city, which
was founded, as Saint Augustine observes, by Cain in the name
of his own son *Enoch.* In the opposing natures of Enoch and
Hazel, we have, in a very real sense, representatives of the "two
lines of the human race which from first to last divide it"; for, as
Saint Augustine noted,

> Accordingly, two cities have been formed by two loves: the
> earthly by the love of self, even to the contempt of God; the
> heavenly by the love of God, even to the contempt of self. The
> former, in a word, glories in itself, the latter in the Lord. For the
> one seeks glory from men; but the greatest glory of the other
> is God, the witness of conscience. . . . And therefore the wise
> men of the one city, living according to man, have sought for
> profit to their own bodies or souls, or both, and those who have
> known God "glorified Him not as God, neither were thankful, but
> became vain in their imaginations, and their foolish heart was
> darkened; professing themselves to be wise"—that is, glorying in
> their own wisdom, and being possessed by pride—"they became
> fools, and changed the glory of the incorruptible God into an
> image made like to corruptible man, and to birds, and four-footed
> beasts, and creeping things." For they were either leaders or
> followers of the people in adoring images, "and worshipped and
> served the creature more than the Creator, who is blessed for
> ever." But in the other city there is no human wisdom, but only
> godliness, which offers due worship to the true God, and looks
> for its reward in the society of the saints, of holy angels as well
> as holy men, "that God may be all in all." [9]

IV   *Murders Symbolic and Real*

The final section of *Wise Blood* occurs as a series of violent
and destructive acts, each of which marks the death of some vital

component of Haze's nature and the end of a particular line of development within the novel. The first of these is Haze's abrupt demolition of the shrunken mummy, the gift of Enoch who is convinced that his wise blood has led him to the new jesus. The mummy, clearly symbolic, carries, like Captain Ahab's doubloon, a variety of meanings according to the interpreter. It is, in an objective sense, the residue of man after the removal of the vital principle, literally the "handful of dust," which the materialist insists is the sum of the human essence. Also an oddity, an anomaly, the mummy is displayed in the public museum as an object of scientific interest. Enoch senses at once a mysterious pull emanating from the dwarfish image, and he selects the miniature grotesque for his temporary deity. In this action, Enoch reenacts the role of the primitive worshiper who selects a strange and foreign object as his god. His presentation of the bizarre artifact to Haze is an invitation to partake of idolatry.

It is unlikely, however, that Haze is consciously aware of these various possibilities when he so savagely attacks the mummy. It is offered to him as a token child by Sabbath Lily. In the familiar face she finds the universal child; she identifies herself as its mother and refers to Haze as the "daddy." Her entrance recalls Haze from his own preoccupation with another family relationship. Wearing his mother's glasses, he has been peering into the mirror, out of which his mother's face stares back at him. Undoubtedly, that face recalls to him his lost life, his forsaken identity, the intensity of his former dedication to a now rejected set of ideals. It is, in fact, his own conscience which gazes at him out of the eyes of his dead mother. Of conscience, Haze has said in a public sermon: "Your conscience is a trick . . . it don't exist though you may think it does, and if you think it does, you had best get it out in the open and hunt it down and kill it, because it's no more than your face in the mirror is or your shadow behind you."

His contemplation of the "face in the mirror" is broken by Sabbath Lily's intrusion. In an instant, Haze repudiates Lily and his own association with her. The contrast between his paramour and his own mother and the suggestion of the child which might well be produced by himself and Lily operate as a violent catalyst within him, and he dashes the mummy's sawdust brains out against the wall and flings the shriveled skin out the door. The action also serves as a harsh rejection of Enoch Emery and of his absurd dabblings in idolatry. Finally, Haze "murders" his own conscience, which has been stirred to life by the sight of the lost mother in the mirror. Haze now vows to rid himself of Sabbath Lily and the futile course he has followed in Taulkingham. He announces his intention to go to a new city, find a new woman and a new room, and begin again to preach the truth of his Church Without Christ.

The symbolic murder of the effigy prefigures the actual murder of Solace Layfield, the false twin. Haze goes about this homicide with the same dogged directness with which he had bought a new hat or had wooed the preacher's daughter with the gift of the potato peeler. On a country road he runs over the consumptive prophet, who is frantically shedding his clothes in a desperate attempt to escape the "madman." Haze justifies his act to Solace by explaining: "You ain't true. . . . You believe in Jesus. . . . Two things I can't stand . . . a man that ain't true and one that mocks what is." Haze's act is, of course, a case of self-murder, for Haze is the one who believes in Jesus. Once more he attacks conscience, knowing that "if you don't hunt it down and kill it, it'll hunt you down and kill you."

In preparation for his journey to the new city, Haze has his car readied at the service station. There he confesses his beliefs to the young attendant, who is dubious of the operational efficiency of either the vehicle or the creed. Haze has now renounced blasphemy for a philosophy of total materialism ("it was not right to believe anything you couldn't see or hold in your hands or test with your teeth"). Typically, Haze is unable to act in a manner consistent with his views, for he soon begins again to blaspheme Jesus vigorously. Haze's mission to the new city is cut short, however, by the patrolman who removes Haze from the highway and eliminates his auto as a road menace by disposing of the car over the high embankment. Haze recognizes the patrolman's act as the "sign" he has so long awaited, and his career undergoes at this point a reversal as dramatic as that of Paul struck down on the road to Damascus.

In order to grasp the full significance of the loss of the auto to Haze, we must consider its prior role in his life. With autos, as with women, Haze is an initiate. He barely succeeds in getting the car driven from the car lot; despite the unreliability of the car's mechanical performance, he is a devoted worshiper who is convinced that, "if you have a good car, you don't have to worry." The car is at once Haze's holy ground (he preaches from its nose as had his grandfather before him), his mobile home (he sometimes sleeps in it), and his guarantee of removal to a new place when the old one fails. The car also becomes his death weapon when he kills Solace Layfield. For Haze, as for many modern car owners, the auto becomes literally a projection of his own identity; and the wanton destruction of it by the police officer must be interpreted as a sign from God. After Haze had waited in vain for such a sign as a boy, he had stubbornly continued in his dramatic ritual of self-mortification. Now, after the lawman leaves, Haze proceeds directly to the terrible act of expiation. Having at last seen God, he will look on man no more.

V   A Rich Nothingness

The blinding of Haze, like that of Oedipus, occurs offstage. Our concern is not with the execution of the act but with its meaning. It is, for Haze, the dying into life—the rejection of claims of the body for the demands of the spirit, the cleansing of his outward vision that he may be prepared for the interior illumination. His course of self-mortification does not stop with the sacrifice of his eyes. He continues to atone through other acts of penance, walking abroad daily in shoes lined with rock and broken glass, wrapping barbed wire about his chest that the flesh may expiate in full his infractions of the holy law. He displays a stolid indifference toward the ordinary preoccupations of the human sphere— money, food, and social intercourse no longer have any significance for him. He withdraws literally and psychologically from the world as he enters the *via negativa,* the path of the holy ascetic.

Haze follows intuitively the course outlined by Saint Augustine in the tenth book of the *Confessions,* when he renounces the "lust of the eyes" (by which Saint Augustine refers to all sensory gratifications) for "the light, melody, fragrance, meat, embracement of my inner man" which derive from the love of God. Walter Hilton, the fourteenth-century mystic, speaks of this dying to the world through the total emptying of the senses as "a darkness full of blessing, a rich nothingness." [10]

Mrs. Flood, Haze's landlady, is baffled and disturbed by his enigmatic conduct: he throws his unneeded cash in the waste-basket; he does not smoke or drink and barely notices the special dishes she prepares for him. Haze commits himself to ancient paths of poverty and chastity, and to obedience to a higher law, the "essential virtues of the mystic quest," which lead to total abnegation of self.

Evelyn Underhill explains in *Mysticism* the significance of the traditional vows as follows:

> By *Poverty* the mystic means an utter self-stripping, the casting off of immaterial as well as material wealth, a complete detachment from all finite things. By *Chastity* he means an extreme and limpid purity of soul, cleansed from personal desire and virgin to all but God: by *Obedience,* that abnegation of self-hood, that mortification of the will, which results in a complete self-abandonment, a "holy indifference" to the accidents of life. These three aspects of perfection are really one: linked together as irrevocably as the three aspects of the self. Their common characteristic is this: they tend to make the subject regard itself, not as an isolated and interesting individual, possessing desires and rights, but as a scrap of the Cosmos, an ordinary bit of the Universal Life, only important as a part of the All, an expression of the Will Divine.[11]

Mrs. Flood, on the other hand, is offended by Haze's refusal to acknowledge her personal identity: "She began to enjoy sitting on the porch with him, but she could never tell if he knew she was there or not. Even when he answered her, she couldn't tell if he knew it was she. She herself. Mrs. Flood, the landlady. Not just anybody." Her literal mind refuses enlightenment; for, when Haze explains that he wears the barbed wire because "I'm not clean," [12] she responds, "I know it . . . you got blood on that night shirt and on the bed. You ought to get you a wash-woman." In her literal-mindedness, she is like Enoch, who obligingly answered Hazel's call for a "new jesus" with a palpable image of deity.

Mrs. Flood's vague sense that she is somehow the victim of an unfair hoax is the typical response of the literal mind to the symbolic mode or to the allegorical gesture. Owen Barfield notes on this point:

Listen attentively to the response of a dull or literal mind to what insistently presents itself as allegory or symbol, and you may detect a certain irritation, a faint, incipient aggressiveness in its refusal. . . . You may, for instance, hear the literal man object suspiciously that he is being "got at." And this is quite correct. He is. Just as he is being "got at" by his unconscious through the symbolism of his dreams. An attempt is being made, of which he is dimly aware, to undermine his idols, and his feet are being invited on to the beginning of the long road, which in the end must lead him to self-knowledge, with all the unacceptable humiliations which that involves.[13]

Mrs. Flood herself adheres to a philosophy of total ethical relativism: "I believe that what's right today is wrong tomorrow and that the time to enjoy yourself is now so long as you let others do the same." She constantly interprets Haze's actions in terms of what *she* would have done under like circumstances: "If she had been blind, she would have sat by the radio all day, eating cake and ice cream, and soaking her feet." Mrs. Flood, like so many of O'Connor's characters, is trapped in the *self* which she assumes is the center of the cosmos. Hazel's path, by contrast, is one of total rejection of selfhood, so that he may prepare a perfect gift for God.

Mrs. Flood also objects that Haze's wire shirt is anachronistic:

"Well, it's not normal. It's like one of them gory stories. It's something that people have quit doing—like boiling in oil or being a saint or walling up cats," she said. "There's no reason for it. People have quit doing it."
"They ain't quit doing it as long as I'm doing it," he said.

As far as she is concerned, Haze "might as well be one of them monks . . . he might as well be in a monkery." And she is right, for Haze is following ancient patterns of salvation which his soul intuitively discovers according to his need. The anchorites who fled to the desert, the solitaries who systematically emptied their senses that they might focus fully on the single divine truth, the martyrs who suffered in the extreme to testify to their belief— these various patterns are adopted by Haze, who is determined to expunge his impurities through superhuman efforts so that he may adequately redeem himself before the God he has so deeply betrayed.

But Mrs. Flood, blind to Haze's spiritual motives, finally concludes (like some early readers of the story) that Haze is insane;
and she formulates the plan of marrying him as a solution of
mutual benefit: he will enjoy the ministrations of a person of
sense; she will at last have full access to his monthly check from
the government. But Haze does not wait to hear the end of her
proposal; he departs abruptly into the frigid outdoors, where the
wind slashes "like sharp knives swirling in the air." It is as if
Haze feels he must surrender his last vestige of earthly comfort—
his warm room and the care of a sympathetic attendant—in order
to demonstrate his total renunciation of earthly concerns. He is
discovered a few days later dying in a drainage ditch. When he
asks where he is, the cop gives him a friendly whack on the head,
and Haze dies quietly in the back of the squad car.

When the body is delivered to Mrs. Flood, she fails to notice
that he has expired and continues weaving their future together.
When she at last becomes aware that Haze seems to have disappeared entirely into the dark tunnel with the light at the end,
"She shut her eyes and saw the pin point of light but so far
away that she could not hold it steady in her mind. She felt as if
she were blocked at the entrance of something. She sat staring
with her eyes shut, into his eyes, and felt as if she had finally got
to the beginning of something she couldn't begin, and she saw
him moving farther and farther away, farther and farther into
the darkness until he was the pin point of light." Mrs. Flood is
attracted to the mysterious realm where light shines in the midst
of darkness, but she is "blocked at the entrance," for, to the
suppliant who is denied the gift of grace, God dwells ever in
"light inaccessible" (1 Tim. 6:16).

VI A Divine Paradox

The final meaning of Hazel Motes's actions has given rise to
considerable critical concern. In theological terms, it might be
maintained that Hazel Motes, as a recipient of sanctifying grace,
performs an act approaching perfect contrition; thus his soul,
through active justification, possibly attains grace even without
the final sacrament of penance. However, such an interpretation
opens many areas of doctrinal controversy, and it is probably too
strongly reliant on specifically Catholic dogma. What is important

—and fully evident—is that Haze sins, suffers, and is undoubtedly redeemed—at least in the terms in which he is presented within the story.[14] Some readers object, however, that Haze's act is too extreme and is insufficiently motivated. But Haze is guilty of blasphemy, murder, and sexual impurity. His rigorous fundamentalist-Puritan heritage would insist upon an extreme act of expiation if he is to be saved from everlasting damnation. That Haze would perform heavy penance, once he admits the sacrilegious nature of his past conduct, is indicated by the acts of self-punishment he committed when he was a boy.

Although Haze's conduct strikes many modern readers as verging on the lunatic, Christian history is filled with examples of similar radical testimonies to faith. Haze's participation in acute suffering as a means of transcending the impurities of the flesh is striking and suggests many historic—and mythic—parallels. Haze, indeed, is the divine paradox, the Christian despite himself. The novel makes many unaccustomed demands upon the reader, primarily through the fusion of highly disparate elements. It is, among other things, almost a burlesque set within a theological frame. What emerges is comedy in the sense of providing laughter that we may be reminded of our vices; it is tragedy in the sense that it deals with the recurring enigma of the human soul seeking its divine destiny. It is realism in that the implied attitudes are fleshed in palpable human embodiments which enact specific gestures on a concrete stage. Yet, the ideas extend toward allegory and carry implications buried in, and expressed through, both action and performer. The paradoxical method reflects the dualism at the center of Christian doctrine—the incarnation, whereby divinity is made flesh. On the one hand, we are reminded of the frailties to which the body unilluminated by the Holy Spirit is liable—on the other, of the scale of transcendence possible to the recipient of grace.

Ten years after the first publication of *Wise Blood*, Flannery O'Connor added the following statement as an introduction to the second edition:

Wise Blood has reached the age of ten and is still alive. . . . It is a comic novel about a Christian *malgré lui*, and as such, very serious, for all comic novels that are any good must be about matters of life and death. *Wise Blood* was written by an author congenitally innocent of theory, but one with certain preoccupations. That belief in Christ is to some a matter of life and death has been a stumbling block for readers who would prefer to think it a matter of no great consequence. For them Hazel Motes' integrity lies in his trying with such vigor to get rid of the ragged figure who moves from tree to tree in the back of his mind. For the author Hazel's integrity lies in his not being able to. Does one's integrity ever lie in what he is not able to do? I think that usually it does, for free will does not mean one will, but many wills conflicting in one man. Freedom cannot be conceived simply. It is a mystery and one which a novel, even a comic novel, can only be asked to deepen.

CHAPTER *4*

Excursions into Catastrophe

WISE BLOOD presents in Hazel Motes a favorite O'Connor figure—the man brought to God by direct intervention of the Holy Spirit. Three stories of the first collection, *A Good Man Is Hard to Find and Other Stories* (1955), illustrate a second of O'Connor's major narrative patterns: the apathetic subject exposed to violent assault by a human agent as a divine stratagem to force the "victim" to grace or spiritual illumination. Hulga, of "Good Country People," must be robbed of her most valued possession—the wooden leg which is at once the sign of her differentness and evidence of the spurious nature of her intellectual convictions—as a rude instruction in the reality of evil. Mrs. Cope ("A Circle in the Fire") must be deprived of a portion of her precious property by her youthful "demonic" visitants, who prove to be avenging angels in disguise. She must lose her "place" (both "property" and sense of "position") in order that she may discover her common bond with dispossessed humanity and thus come to a renewed sense of her own identity. And the grandmother of "A Good Man Is Hard to Find" must be brought to the brink of catastrophe before she forgets her obsessive self-concern in a splendid moment of selfless compassion.

In addition to their depiction of salvation through disaster, these three stories also have other interesting features in common. The protagonist of each is a female character (the three together span the full spectrum of the generations). Each story begins with the presentation of a close-knit family unit or of a combination family-economic group which is itself beset by deep inner tensions. Into each of these closed groups a stranger (or strangers) intrudes, posing a threat which is ultimately fulfilled by his divesting the protagonist of what she most prizes (material possessions, life, or limb) but, in the process, freeing her to attain or at least move toward grace through forcing her to the acceptance of a new identity.

I *Where Nothing Is: "Good Country People"*

"Good Country People" takes as its theme the archetypal encounter of innocence and experience. The curious "twist" which
makes the story unique within its category is that the initiate
(Hulga Hopewell) is a thirty-two-year-old lady Ph.D. who assumes that her formal education prepares her to recognize evil
in all its guises—she has, in fact, arrived at the supreme insight:
everything is nothing. Her ultimate instructor in corruption is
Manley Pointer, a backwoods collector of the unusual and the
obscure who is masked as a Bible salesman. Through her rude
initiation, Hulga discovers that the realities of experience outrun
all possibilities of metaphysical speculation.

Actually, there are three "worlds" within the story presented
or implied: the farm, the university, and the back country. Together, the three form a hierarchy of intellectual sophistication
and worldliness. The Bible salesman's unexpected action at
the end upsets the hierarchy by exposing the gaping discrepancy
between supposition and fact; when he runs away with the artificial leg, he is, in fact, seizing the prize that declares him the
victor in life's game of multileveled deception.

The first "world"—the farm where the action of the story occurs
—constitutes (in its owner's view) the *norm* for human conduct
and attitudes. Joy (Hulga) and Manley are defined as aberrants
by the standards of "normality," for one is too "intellectual" and
the other too "simple." The farm, on the other hand, affirms the
via media, the *literal view* of reality. It gives primacy to the
realm of fact, to the familiar details of human biology and social
experience. Mrs. Freeman's talk is limited to faithful reports of
Carramae's pregnancy or the talents of Glynese's boyfriend, an
aspiring chiropractor, who pops her neck to cure a sty. Religion
is relegated to the attic and is seldom referred to except in properly sanctimonious attitudes. Philosophy is limited to a familiar
round of banal observations that serve to explain all circumstance
and account for all exigencies: "Nothing is perfect . . . that is life!
. . . well, other people have their opinions, too." The farm, a world
of Edenic seclusion, is untroubled, therefore, by niceties of
philosophic questioning or theological probing. Its attitudes, its
ideas—like its daily routines and conversations—are fixed and continue in a comfortable pattern of unbroken repetition.

When Joy (Hulga), because of her weak heart (a significant symptom), returns to the farm from the "great world" of the university to live among these provincials, her scorn is boundless. Having failed in her attempted escape, she now displays her contempt by a studied series of irritating mannerisms and withering comments. She stomps about the house to remind her mother of her daughter's painful deformity; she changes her name from "Joy" to "Hulga," apparently because the latter is the ugliest she can discover; and she repeatedly undercuts the obtuse Mrs. Freeman. Joy's academic attainments have left her totally unsuited for the life of the farm. Joy's doctorate, like her change of name, signals her renunciation of her old environment and her intent to claim a new role. Mrs. Hopewell, however, is perplexed by this new identity, just as she is puzzled by many aspects of Joy's behavior: "You could say, 'My daughter is a nurse,' or 'My daughter is a school teacher,' or even, 'My daughter is a chemical engineer.' You could not say, 'My daughter is a philosopher.' That was something that had ended with the Greeks and Romans."

Despite Joy's airs of intellectual superiority, Mrs. Hopewell continues to regard her as a mere child. And Mrs. Hopewell also enjoys a keen sense of her own inner worth: "Mrs. Hopewell had no bad qualities of her own but she was able to use other people's in such a constructive way that she never felt the lack." As for Mrs. Freeman, she "could never be brought to admit herself wrong on any point." The story is, among other things, an excursion into the follies bred of vanity and pride.

Manley Pointer, the backwoods Bible salesman, serves to complete the hierarchy of intellect. He is from far back in the country, "not even from a place, just near a place." Far from giving himself "airs," he humbly insists upon his innocence and accuses Mrs. Hopewell of disliking him for it: "I know I'm real simple. I don't know how to say a thing but to say it. I'm just a country boy. . . . People like you don't like to fool with country people like me!" Manley piously asserts that he wishes to devote his life to "Chrustian service."

The game played out between Manley and Mrs. Hopewell is a foreshadowing of the later game of seduction between Manley and Hulga, and in each instance, the deception extends to both sides. Mrs. Hopewell, who pretends to approve of Manley's rural innocence, proves her goodwill by asking him to dinner—an invitation she immediately regrets. She also lies to him by insisting that her Bible is in the bedroom, instead of confessing that her atheist daughter has forced her to banish the book from sight. When Hulga sets in motion her cunning plan of seduction, she assumes that she is preparing a union of total sophistication (herself) with total innocence (Manley). She is prepared to deal with Manley's inevitable guilts after the consummation of the event: "She imagined that she took his remorse in hand and changed it to a deeper understanding of life. She took all his shame away and turned it into something useful." In the barn loft, Hulga explains her philosophy: "I'm one of those people who see *through* to nothing. . . . We are all damned . . . but some of us have taken off our blindfolds and see there's nothing to see. It's a kind of salvation." To make their relationship completely "honest," she confesses she is really thirty (actually, she is thirty-two).

Hulga intends to play intellectual Eve to this untouched Adam. However, she soon discovers that the country boy is not so simple as he appears. The rustic has come prepared for the outing with whiskey, contraceptives, and a pack of pornographic cards which he produces from his hollow Bible (the analogue of Hulga's false leg). Indeed, Hulga is rapidly undeceived as to his true character. When she pleads, "Aren't you . . . just good country people?" he replies: "I hope you don't think that I believe in that crap! I may sell Bibles but I know which end is up and I wasn't born yester-day and I know where I'm going!"

Manley Pointer seems well named for his role in the promised union. He is, as well, a connoisseur of the obscene and adds Hulga's leg to his growing collection of bizarre objects. Hulga's venture into sexual initiation leads her to spiritual rape. As Manley pops the leg into his valise, he sneers a final taunt: "And I'll tell you another thing, Hulga . . . you ain't so smart. I been be-lieving in nothing ever since I was born!" Then he leaves Hulga immobilized in the loft, to contemplate the meaning of her ex-perience. Hulga is abruptly hurled, therefore, from the intel-lectual heights she had so smugly inhabited; Manley is exposed as a disguised villain. Mrs. Hopewell and Mrs. Freeman are left unchanged in their usual state of self-satisfied ignorance. Mrs. Hopewell, viewing the salesman fleeing across the meadows, reflects, "He was so simple . . . but I guess the world would be better off if we were all that simple."

In one sense, "Good Country People" is a variation on the traditional frontier story of the trade or swap. The frontier audience was especially responsive to this kind of tale in which a duel of wits occurs between two "double-dealers" who contend for the prize of horse or whiskey. Disguise and deception were not denounced as a swindler's device but were applauded as the clever weapons by which one maneuvered to victory in the game which reflected in little the struggle for survival on the primitive frontier. Davy Crockett, for example, sells his coonskin a dozen times to the unsuspecting barkeeper who obligingly supplies whiskey for the crowd at each exchange. The emphasis is obviously on Davy's intellectual shrewdness rather than on his equivocal ethics; the frontier audience, delighted by his success, obligingly ignores his violation of the common codes of honest behavior.

Our reaction to the outcome of "Good Country People" is comparable to that aroused by the frontier duel of wits. Manley is the victor in the game of mutual deceit, and the leg is his trophy. Hulga has been outsmarted by a country bumpkin; she has lost her position of intellectual superiority along with her leg. Although she has won our sympathies, we feel at the same time a secret glow of inner satisfaction to see the clever know-it-all bested by a backwoods ignoramus.

Here, as elsewhere in Flannery O'Connor, what distinguishes the modern version of the frontier tale is that her events do not occur in a moral vacuum. Hulga is judged as pride overthrown, but Manley reminds us that pure evil persists in the world in all its vulgar attributes, whether we know it or not. One does not have to take a Ph.D. to become the devil's disciple. Depravity and its rituals are easily learned without benefit of seminar or graduate lecture. And it is to be hoped that Hulga, having mastered the fundamentals of the fact of evil, is now prepared for additional instruction in spiritual reality.

II   *Burnt Offering: "A Circle in the Fire"*

"A Circle in the Fire," like "Good Country People," utilizes the motif of the intruder who delivers a harsh lesson to an un-

willing pupil. To some extent, we react toward Mrs. Cope with
the same ambivalence of feeling we experienced for Hulga. On
the one hand, we sympathize with the widow's struggle to maintain her holdings against the "diabolic" invaders. On the other
hand, we sense in her fall possible divine retribution against one
who has forgotten the biblical injunction against laying up
treasures on earth.

Mrs. Cope, the proprietress of a productive farm, is so involved
with her own material concerns that she is oblivious to the human
needs of those about her. She views her helpers as so many
economic ciphers, potential contributors to her own welfare.
They, in turn, devise means to ignore or subvert her materialistic
interests. Only with the advent of the uninvited children is Mrs.
Cope shocked into the discovery that a pious industry does not
insure invulnerability against the misfortunes that beset the common ranks of man.

Mrs. Cope's employees do not share her zealous dedication to
her own prosperity. Mrs. Pritchard takes refuge in a morbid preoccupation with death and misfortune. She will travel thirty miles
for a funeral, and she speculates lasciviously as to how conception
takes place in an iron lung. When the children arrive at the farm,
Mrs. Pritchard brightens noticeably at the prospect of a break
in the dull routine and the likely confirmation of all her pes-
simistic views of life. The black helpers, who have little to lose
or gain by the vicissitudes of Mrs. Cope's fortunes, shuffle about
their duties doggedly oblivious to her pleas for efficiency and
thrift. They are on the farm, but not of it. They could be replaced
as easily as a piece of broken machinery or a withered plant. To
Mrs. Cope, they are "as destructive and impersonal as the nut
grass," which itself is like "an evil sent directly by the devil to
destroy the place."

Mrs. Cope, like the black workers, is deaf to the demands of
those about her. While the youngsters blurt out their piteous
description of life in the Atlanta development, her mind is busy
with premonitions of fires and lawsuits for injury. Mrs. Cope is
inordinately proud of her "place," the farm she so carefully
nurtures to productiveness. What she fails to grasp is that her
unexpected visitors are children without place: they are outcasts
in a world which affords them little material benefit and less love.
Powell, the spokesman of the group, explains matter-of-factly that

his father is now dead; his mother has remarried, and he now lives "out to one of them developments" in Atlanta. The general tenor of life in the development is glimpsed through the smallest boy's description: "The only way you can tell your own is by smell. . . . They're four stories high and there's ten of them, one behind the other." In the midst of this urban hell, Powell has never forgotten the lost rural paradise: "Listen here . . . all the time we been knowing him [Powell] he's been telling us about this here place. Said it was everything here. Said it was horses here. Said he had the best time of his entire life right here on this here place."

Mrs. Hopewell's daughter, Sally Virginia, is a counterpoint both to her mother and the boys. She watches the unannounced arrival of the children silently from the upstairs window and later spies on them in the woods. The child both opposes and identifies with her mother. "Leave me be," she cries on departing for the woods. "I ain't you." But, when Powell and his friends set the woods on fire, she dashes frantically to the house to sound the alarm. As yet, she is unable to interpret the meaning of what she has witnessed, even on a literal level. Her screams refer to plans for a parking lot, not a fire. The child regards the boys as pure evil. She continually boasts that she herself would give them short shrift. Mrs. Cope would undoubtedly like to resort to such direct measures, but she equivocates: she neither totally accepts nor openly rejects the boys. This equivocation (she is a woman neither completely good nor totally bad) has characterized her life, and it now becomes her undoing. The children, who are not inhibited by the ethical and practical restraints usually governing adult action, now enact with the fire what are probably the secret desires of Mrs. Cope's helpers, who have little reason to care whether her property is preserved or destroyed.

When the boys move into action, they are as inexorable as a natural force. Their "meanness" would support an argument for innate depravity, in the view of those who advocate the sanctity of personal property as a moral absolute. The story, however, is an attack upon precisely just such attitudes. Mrs. Cope, in her absorption with personal holdings, has lost touch with her less fortunate brethren. In her press for possessions, she has lost sight of charity.

The *circle* with which the story closes has been anticipated through earlier imagery. When the blacks drive the tractor in the wrong direction, Mrs. Pritchard attracts their attention by swinging her arm in a fierce circle. Powell's wavering eye seems to enclose the entire farm "in one encircling stare." Indeed, Mrs. Cope sees the farm residents as a little circle of humanity with herself at the center. It is this vision—of a self enclosing all within its range, or of a world where all needs are peripheral except one's own—which is broken irrevocably for Mrs. Cope. As she views the flames consuming her land, her face wears the look of a "new misery"—a look that "might have belonged to anybody, a Negro or a European or to Powell himself." Meanwhile, the children are dancing in the woods, with "wild high shrieks of joy as if the prophets were dancing in the fiery furnace, in the circle the angel had cleared for them." However, Mrs. Cope's physical loss represents ultimate spiritual gain. Through the acts of the children, she is divested of pride and learns her own true position in the ranks of a fallen humanity.

III *One of My Babies: "A Good Man Is Hard to Find"*

"A Good Man Is Hard to Find," like the two stories just considered, treats of an encounter with a "mysterious stranger." The difference is, however, that the hapless family in this tale ventures forth into the precarious world for the disastrous meeting, and the confrontation is vastly more serious in its issues. According to O'Connor, the story is intended to demonstrate the efficacious operation of grace in extremity. On another level, however, the events suggest the disturbing possibility of a contrary—even nihilistic—interpretation.

As in the other stories, the opening action reveals a close group beset by tensions among the various members. The grandmother nags insistently at her taciturn son (Bailey) who masks his annoyance in stubborn silence. Her constant lecturing to her grandchildren evokes a stream of sassy rebuttal, but the grandmother gamely ignores the various rebukes and secretly connives to get her own way as much as possible. The children add to the confusion by arguing with each other, and at one point they almost upset the car in their frenzied efforts to get their father to turn off the highway toward the old plantation.

The tension which has been introduced through the family

antagonisms and reinforced through the various references to the homicidal maniac who is known to be at large in the area is unleashed in full force when the car flips into the ditch and the murderers materialize on the horizon. From this point on, the situation is one of crisis, as this "typical" American family undergoes a highly untypical end, for the grandmother has brought the family to disaster. Her petty selfishness has caused them to detour off the main road to search for the misplaced plantation, just as she, through her stubborn willfulness, has placed the cat in position ready to spring onto Bailey's neck and to precipitate the accident. The wreck throws the grandmother into the front section, where she huddles under the dashboard, hoping she is hurt so "Bailey's wrath would not come down on her all at once."

The grandmother seals the family's fate when she blurts out her recognition of the Misfit, the maniac who now stands before them. Typically, the grandmother attempts to forestall the gunman's violence with conversation. She pleads with him on religious grounds, appeals to his family background, and offers him money and clothing. The Misfit, in turn, participates willingly in the dialogue. He vows that he did, in fact, come from an upright mother and father; and he even apologizes for appearing before a lady without a shirt. Two matters, in particular, trouble the Misfit. Like a Kafka hero, he cannot remember the crime of which he stands convicted. The prison psychiatrist has told him that he killed his father, but whether this act was literal or symbolic is not made clear. The outlaw insists upon his innocence: "My daddy died in nineteen ought nineteen of the epidemic flu and I never had a thing to do with it." He is also distressed by Christ's claims to have raised the dead: "It ain't right I wasn't there because if I had of been there I would have known." The Misfit concludes that one has only two real choices: to believe in Christ and follow Him, or to deny Christ and pursue a life of evil. Through the Misfit's words, O'Connor by implication indicts all who refuse either to affirm or deny, choosing instead to drift aimlessly in the ambiguous realms of the trimmer.[1]

The grandmother, shaken at last from her total self-preoccupation, experiences a moment of compassion just before she is shot: "Why you're one of my babies. You're one of my own children!" In O'Connor's words, this final impulse of selflessness is evidence that the old lady has at last been admitted to grace: "it is the

free act, the acceptance of grace particularly, that I always have
my eye on as the thing which will make the story work. In the
story 'A Good Man Is Hard to Find,' it is the grandmother's
recognition that the Misfit is one of her children. . . ." [2]
Admittedly, several problems arise when we consider the ultimate meaning of this story. Surely, the grandmother's final transcendence of self in her last moments is admirable, but death
on such terms as she encounters seems a high price to pay for
salvation. The Misfit avers, "She would of been a good woman . . .
if it had been somebody there to shoot her every minute of her
life." In O'Connor's view, there seems to be no place in the
divine scheme for human imperfection. The common frailties of
humanity are unacceptable, and the imperfect specimen deserves
to be damned for his failings or blasted to salvation by a final
insurgence of grace that is produced in an extreme moment.[3]

The Misfit poses even more complex problems of interpretation.
The grandmother recognizes him as someone long familiar, a face
she has known all her life. Is his the face of a fallen humanity
which has rejected the authority of Christ's testimony for the
seductive pleasures of a life dedicated to evil? Possibly, but even
the Misfit renounces his earlier endorsement of the evil-pleasure
principle in his final statement that "It's no real pleasure in life."
In his role as the prisoner condemned to a life sentence for crimes
he cannot recall, the Misfit inevitably suggests the plight of all
suffering humanity that is burdened with guilt for unremembered
transgressions. The charge of murdering the father recalls both
the crime of Oedipus and the slaying of Christ. Yet the Misfit
specifically identifies *himself* with Christ, who also "thown
everything off balance." The Misfit seems to act both as divine
avenger and as diabolic assailant. He is at once the emblem of a
society which has rejected Christ and the instrument by which
that society is apprehended.

The killing of the parent is a prominent theme in O'Connor, but
the significance of the act is always highly ambiguous. On the
one hand, the failures of the parent lead to the conclusion that
he deserves annihilation (for sins of pride, selfhood, pettiness).
The "executioner," however, is frequently left with an overwhelming burden of guilt and remorse after he realizes his own
failure of understanding and compassion.[4] Likewise, we can see
in this story that the grandmother's *pride* can be uprooted only

through violent means. Yet, at the same time, we feel that she is unfairly subjected to excessive violence. Indeed, the wholesale slaughter of the grandmother and her family through their chance meeting with a maniacal stranger might well support a nihilistic world view.

Despite its theological perplexities, the story stands among the finest in the O'Connor canon. The movement from the tensions of comedy to those of tragedy is swift and inexorable. The meeting of the grandmother and the Misfit is at once improbable and persuasive. Whether read as Christian testimony or a nihilistic document, the story is powerful in its impact. The final dialogue, whether we accept or reject its assertions, poses many of the significant issues which occupy the philosophic consciousness of the age.

Stories such as "Good Country People," "A Circle in the Fire," and "A Good Man Is Hard to Find" are studies in pride over-thrown, of the downfall of a heady conceit that suddenly dis-covers its vulnerability to the unforeseen "malevolence" which assails the world. Joy, Mrs. Cope, the grandmother—all are con-vinced of their inner capacity to deal with reality—to handle the contingencies of their life experience—until they are suddenly confronted with forces more powerful than themselves. The country Bible salesman, the capricious youngsters, and the insane criminal prove to be more than a match for their arrogant victims. For Flannery O'Connor, the instruction of pride through the les-sons of humility is, in each story, the means by which the soul is prepared for its necessary illumination by the Holy Spirit.

CHAPTER *5*

Sacraments Violated and Mysteries Confronted

THAT Flannery O'Connor subscribed to a deeply sacramental view of life in all its aspects is everywhere evident in her work. In a talk at Notre Dame in 1957, she said that "The Catholic sacramental view of life is one that maintains and supports at every turn the vision that the story teller must have if he is going to write fiction of any depth." [1] Strongly involved with her vision of life as sacrament is the corollary recognition of the *mystery* that everywhere pervades human experience. For her, a story is worth writing and reading because of "what is left over after everything explainable has been explained. . . . The writer's gaze has to extend beyond the surface, beyond mere problems, until it touches that realm of mystery which is the concern of the prophet." [2]

Five stories in her first collection, *A Good Man Is Hard to Find and Other Stories,* probe the mysteries which enfold the many stages of human action. Three of these—"The River," "A Temple of the Holy Ghost," and "The Life You Save May Be Your Own"—deal specifically with sacraments as such: baptism, Eucharist, and matrimony. Two others—"A Stroke of Good Fortune" and "A Late Encounter with the Enemy"—depict characters who fail to grasp the sacramental nature of two of life's most significant experiences: birth and death.

In all of these stories, the mysteries revolve around the divine irony at the center of reality: drowning into salvation is preferable to life in the midst of corruption; the Holy Spirit is sometimes embodied in the grossest forms of being; the basest sinner is often least aware of his spiritual contamination; the sacramental nature of both birth and death may not be recognized by the prime participants.

[74]

I *A Peculiar Baptism: "The River"*

In "The River," the child (who calls himself Bevel) is exposed to the constant exploitations of a corrupt society. His parents neglect him, farming him out to unfamiliar baby-sitters while they sleep off the hangovers which inevitably follow their evening socializings. On mornings when no hired attendant appears, the child is left to fend for himself. He breakfasts on leftovers from the parties of the night before, anchovy and crackers washed down by stale gingerale. The parents' neglect of the physical well-being of their child is paralleled by their unconcern for his spiritual welfare. Seeing a picture of Jesus for the first time, he fails to recognize Him. Ignorant of the basic principles of religious instruction, he does not even know the meaning of the act of baptism.

His parents are unconcerned but not brutal, for their neglect is a result of indifference rather than of active malevolence. At the baby-sitter's, the boy experiences a more active form of exploitation. The other children trick him into letting the hog out of his pen, and the animal pursues the terrified child, butting and mauling him until he escapes to the house. These devilish urchins seem to share with the Misfit the conviction that there is no pleasure in the world except in meanness. After their cruel trick on the unsuspecting visitor, they feel better: "Their stern faces didn't brighten any but they seemed to become less taut, as if some great need had been partly satisfied."

The most sinister of the child's attackers is, of course, Mr. Paradise, the unbeliever. A conspicuous scoffer at the claims of the country preacher, Mr. Paradise pursues the child with a depraved intention.[3] Paradise bounds into the water after the boy "like a giant pig." For, as we have already observed, man, by rejecting the divine principle, reduces himself to the level of the beast. The Reverend Bevel Summers warned that man must choose either Jesus or the devil (his message strongly resembles those of both the Misfit and Hazel Motes); and Mr. Paradise, who has renounced the former, clearly is committed to the latter.

The irony of the child's response to the sermon is that he accepts at full value the literal truth of the preacher's statements. The Reverend Bevel Summers proclaims that the river moves "toward the kingdom of Christ." "There ain't but one river, and that's the River of Life, made out of Jesus' Blood. That's the river you have to lay your pain in, in the River of Faith, in the River of Life, in the River of Love, in the rich red river of Jesus' Blood, you people!" The child perceives that the preacher is serious about his message, despite the fact that, for his parents, life is a meaningless jest in which man is reduced to a nonentity and human existence has no more purpose than a continuing round of cocktail parties.

For the preacher, life has a purposeful relation to a divine principle which resides outside the human sphere; but the child responds only to the literal level of the preacher's assertions. As a result, the course of his action is clear: he rejects his parents, his home (he takes no suitcase because there is nothing there he wants) and, in fact, the world. He sets out to baptize himself, "to keep on going this time until he found the kingdom of Christ in the river." O'Connor has observed that young Bevel's "peculiar desire to find the kingdom of Christ" represents the "working of grace for him." [4] And, since he dies in a state of grace (no conscious act of suicide is committed), he is eligible for direct admission to that kingdom which he seeks: "Bevel hasn't reached the age of reason; therefore he can't commit suicide. He comes to a good end. He's saved from those nutty parents, a fate worse than death. He's been baptized and so he goes to his Maker; this is a good end." [5] Mr. Paradise, his would-be attacker, is left stranded in the earthly stream, "like some ancient water monster" out of a world anterior to the incarnation and the blessing of grace.

O'Connor thus asserts that the child's death, though shocking, is preferable to the meaningless, corrupt existences of those who surround him. His is the dying into life; theirs, the futile death-in-life. Better that the spirit should find its release through violent transformation than endure the living hell of exile from the divine center. The lesson is a difficult one for the modern reader to accept, for the question inevitably arises as to whether or not one can be sure that the act carries significance beyond that of the futile destruction of an unfortunate child-victim. Once again, salvation seems to carry a rather high price tag; but, in the author's eyes at least, redemption is well worth the cost.

O'Connor has explained that one of her basic purposes is to startle the modern audience out of its overwhelming apathy and to reawaken its sense of the "awful mystery" which pervades all human experience: "When I write a novel in which the central action is baptism, I know that for the larger percentage of my readers, baptism is a meaningless rite; therefore I have to imbue this action with an awe and terror which will suggest its awful mystery. I have to distort the look of the thing in order to represent as I see them both the mystery and the fact." [6]

II *The Spirit Made Flesh: "A Temple of the Holy Ghost"*

"The River" reveals the enduring significance of the sacrament of baptism. The central concern of "A Temple of the Holy Ghost" is with the mystery of incarnation, in particular as that mystery is reflected in both the infusion of the human *corpus* with the divine spirit and the celebration of the Incarnation of the Son through the sacrament of the Eucharist. The circus freak serves as a pointed reminder of the vast discrepancy that so often exists between word and flesh, ideal and physical embodiment. This botched specimen hardly seems an apt receptacle for the Holy Spirit. Yet, the freak is merely at the far end of a spectrum of human imperfections, all of which clearly indicate failure of the human embodiment to conform to the ideal concept. Alonzo, the obese local cab driver with his pungent body odors; Miss Kirby, the school teacher-boarder, and her eccentric suitor Mr. Cheatam; the giggling girls from the convent school; the young men studying to be Church of God preachers because these don't have to know anything; the child with her wild fantasies of martyrdom who cannot remember to say her prayers properly—all are, according to orthodox views, temples of the Holy Spirit, residences for the sacred energy which unites man with the essence of the divine. Yet, in each instance, the disparity between the ideal and the reality is so marked that rational explanation is impossible and logical interpretation difficult.

The story, presented through the child's point of view, relates to the discovery of this central paradox as part of her initiation into adult status. The theme of knowledge as such is important throughout the story; it is emphasized by the fact that the girls are in residence at a convent school, where they are presumably students of the mysteries which underlie existence. Likewise, the family boarder is a teacher, but she seems incapable of instructing anyone on any topic of importance. The child is contemptuous of the girls because of their limited intellectual capabilities, just as she is scornful of the young male callers because of their devotion to stupidity as a way of life.

The child obtains her account of the circus freak through an exchange of information, but hers is, of course, totally fraudulent. After hearing of the hermaphrodite's appearance at the sideshow, the child is confronted with the limitations of human knowledge: for no one can offer a lucid, logical explanation for the freak's existence. The horror of the freak's condition seemingly points to a less than benevolent responsible overseer. When reason fails, faith supplies the equivocal answer that "it is God's will." No statement beyond this is possible without rejecting the basic assumptions of belief, that the universe is powered by a just deity beneficent in His attitudes toward man.

The freak's puzzling affliction—an abnormal fusion of both male and femal sexual characteristics—emphasizes the traditional affinity of "knowledge" as such with specifically sexual enlightenment. The hermaphrodite's condition suggests some primordial life form predating the emergence of a two-sex species. To observe the freak is to glimpse one of the ancient mysteries of creation itself. The child's wonder at hearing the story is akin to that aroused by the journey into the circle of whale-mothers in *Moby Dick*. And the child's actual discovery of sexual meaning is similar to that experienced by the child in Katherine Anne Porter's "The Grave," who recognizes a revealed mystery in the unborn rabbits exposed in the dead mother's stomach and intuitively senses that such secret revelations are not to be spoken of.

Closely allied to the themes of "mystery" and of "knowledge" is the notion of conversion or transformation. Many such examples of significant change in appearance or essence occur throughout this story. The young girls, for example, arrive in the drab convent uniforms which they quickly discard for flashier attire; this change of costume suggests the tension between the ideal toward which the nuns are striving to mold their characters and their natural bent for creaturely concerns. Before they return to the convent, the girls dutifully resume their drab garments, in preparation for return to a life which is to them, above all, *dull* in all its attributes. The spiritual teaching of the nuns is likewise converted by the girls to something trivial and ludicrous. Instructed by their mentors that they are temples of the Holy Ghost, the girls thereafter refer to each other as "temple one" and "temple two." The nun's solemn advice on how to preserve their virginity is a constant source of amusement to the giggling pupils. The nuns vainly attempt to impose some pattern of divine significance upon the girls' lives, but so far they seem to have made little headway toward any actual transformation.

The child, who is the point-of-view character, is aware of both the deficiencies everywhere apparent on the human scene and the attractions inherent in the divine example. The child explodes with laughter when she contemplates the inept Mr. Cheatam in the role of suitor; she scoffs at the ignorance of the guitar-strumming country boys; and she suspects the motives of the nuns at the convent. Yet she is enamored of martyrdom; and in a Walter Mitty-like vision, she views herself in the role of consecrated victim:

> She began to prepare her martyrdom, seeing herself in a pair of tights in a great arena, lit by the early Christians hanging in cages of fire, making a gold dusty light that fell on her and the lions. The first lion charged forward and fell at her feet, converted. A whole series of lions did the same. The lions liked her so much she even slept with them and finally the Romans were obliged to burn her but to their astonishment she would not burn down and finding she was so hard to kill, they finally cut off her head very quickly with a sword and she went immediately to heaven.

The child's fantasy is absurd, but it does reveal an awareness of martyrdom as an ideal in human life. In contrast, none of her associates in the secular world, whether adult or child, devotes much thought to the notion of sacrifice for principle as a way of being.

The most significant episode in the transformation sequence occurs in the convent chapel during the celebration of the Eucharist, a ceremony in which the divine essence is presumed to enter into the consecrated materials, thereby literally transforming them into holy substance. The child's illumination about, or at least confrontation with, mystery occurs at the precise moment of the elevation of the Host, when the Divine Man is present. The sacrament of the Eucharist forcefully recalls the mystery of incarnation, the enigma of God become flesh; and it reaffirms the human role in the divine scheme, man's participation in divinity. This dual significance of the ritual is stressed in one of the preliminary prayers: "O God, who in creating human nature, didst wonderfully dignify it, and hast still more wonderfully renewed it; grant that, by the mystery of this water and wine, we may be made partakers of his divinity who vouchsafed to become partaker of our humanity, Jesus Christ. . . ." [7]

Through grace, God extends to man possibilities of salvation. As a creature capable of such redemption, man is more than flesh, greater than matter animated. The child's witnessing of the miracle revives for her the memory of the freak in the sideshow display and of his admonishing his audience of "normal" spectators, "I don't dispute hit. This is the way He wanted me to be." The recollection of the freak's words at this precise moment patently identifies him with Christ, and it also reminds us that the mystical body embraces both sexes; for even the bread and wine have been interpreted as symbols of the androgynous nature of the mystical Christ. [8]

On the way home from the convent, Alonzo, whose ears are "pointed almost like a pig's," reveals that the sideshow is gone; it has been closed by the town ministers who disapproved of the inhumane spectacle. The child, moved by her many discoveries in recent days, is "lost in thought." We are not told the specific content of the child's final meditations on her experience, only that the sun in the distance "was a huge red ball like an elevated Host drenched in blood."

Nothing in the story suggests that the narrative is intended to be other than a presentation of one of God's mysteries. It sets forth the central paradox of creation, the embodiment of ideal spiritual essence in the imperfect human receptacle. The emphasis is upon human deficiencies of various kinds, but none falls clearly into the category of pure evil. The girls from Mount Scholastica fail because of their essentially trivial self-expression; Miss Kirby and her suitor are absurd in their romantic pursuits; the child is limited by inner perversity and outward failures; Alonzo is physically repulsive, as is the man-woman at the fair. No overt attempt is made to reconcile fact with dogma, to adjust the seeming contradiction of experience with the tenets of faith. One is expected to accept the mystery as such, a phenomenon inaccessible to human understanding necessarily restricted by the operation of a limited rationality.

The mystery of the incarnation of the spirit in its variously imperfect human vessels points to what O'Connor has spoken of as the "central Christian mystery: that it [the world] has, for all its horror, been found by God to be worth dying for." [9] But the ultimate impression conveyed by the story does not end here. Inevitably, additional questions are raised as to the responsibility of a cosmic agent which would permit the agony endured by the natural freak. What place does the grotesque human sufferer occupy in the scheme of a benevolent creator? This age-old question of Job carries the implicit indictment of an "omnipotent" ruler whose justice seems to operate with arbitrary cruelty when assessed by human standards. This nihilistic impulse manifestly resides outside the conscious intent of the story itself, but the "demonic" thrust is undeniably there. And, indeed, much of the final appeal of the work is precisely this element of unresolved tension.

III   A Moral Consciousness:
"The Life You Save May Be Your Own"

"The River" deals with the sacrament of baptism, and "A Temple of the Holy Ghost" probes the mystery of the Eucharist; "The Life You Save May Be Your Own" is also concerned with one of the sacred rituals of the church: matrimony and the violation of its sacramental nature by Tom T. Shiftlet who utilizes it merely to serve selfish personal aims. In Mr. Shiftlet, we confront the spectacle of evil presented not as a "problem" but as a "mystery."

This story, like "Good Country People," is structured upon a basic pattern of mutual deception. When a stranger arrives at the farm, the mother, Mrs. Crater, immediately senses the possibility of obtaining a suitable mate for her unpromising offspring Lucynell. Mr. Shiftlet, on the other hand, sees the proposed marriage merely as a way of realizing his long-standing ambition to become an automobile owner. The ceremony concluded, he dumps his bride at a roadside café and continues his journey only slightly troubled by his betrayal.

Closely associated with the theme of deception is the question of human identity and the weaving of one's destiny toward unforeseen ends. In the stranger's initial appearance at the farm, he discourses on the impenetrability of the human spirit: "Lady . . . lemme tell you something. There's one of these doctors in Atlanta that's taken a knife and cut the human heart—the human heart . . . out of a man's chest and held it in his hand . . . and studied it like it was a day-old chicken, and lady . . . he don't know no more about it than you or me."

Queried as to his background, the stranger reflects on the difficulties of establishing human identity: " 'Lady,' he said, 'nowadays, people'll do anything anyways. I can tell you my name is Tom T. Shiftlet and I come from Tarwater, Tennessee, but you never have seen me before: how you know I ain't lying? How you know my name ain't Aaron Sparks, lady, and I come from Singleberry, Georgia, or how you know it's not George Speeds and I come from Lucy, Alabama, or how you know I ain't Thompson Bright from Toolafalls, Mississippi?' "

Indeed, Mr. Shiftlet might well be any of the personages mentioned in his catalogue. Whatever he is, he is not the steady, reliable son-in-law Mrs. Crater seeks as a caretaker for her daughter and as a comfort to her in her old age. Attitudes toward Lucynell (the daughter) also differ: to Mrs. Crater, her imbecile offspring is worth "a casket of jewels." She affirms: "She's smart too. She can sweep the floor, cook, wash, feed the chickens, and hoe." To the youth in the Hot Spot, the sleeping bride is like "an angel of Gawd." Mr. Shiftlet sums up the difficulties inherent in establishing human identity in the conclusion to his self-introduction: "Maybe the best I can tell you is, I'm a man." He then poses the question which is in fact a basic concern of the story: "but listen lady . . . what is a man?" In a very real sense, he voices the problem explored by O'Connor in this story and in all of her other work.

Tom T. Shiftlet, like many of O'Connor's characters, plays a game of deceit to win his own selfish ends. The trick he executes upon Lucynell by marrying and then deserting her shows him capable of an awesome depravity, but the intense corruption of human spirit thus revealed certainly would not be discoverable to the Atlanta doctors in their clinical examination. Mrs. Crater, who is also guilty of deceit in the service of personal ambition, assures Shiftlet that her daughter is fifteen or sixteen, although the unfortunate creature is nearly thirty. Mrs. Crater obviously is aware of the advantages that will accrue to her in the possession of a handyman-carpenter for a son-in-law, for she speculates as to whether a "one-armed man could put a new roof on her garden house." Lucynell is a pawn in the struggle, for each person carefully weighs the advantage to be gained by the bargain.

Mr. Shiftlet asserts that the Atlanta doctor who examined the heart "don't know no more about it than you or me." The true nature of a Shiftlet cannot be fathomed through scientific scrutiny, nor can he be comprehended by the limited mentality of a Mrs. Crater. More important, Mr. Shiftlet, the "shifty" deceiver, is above all self-deceived. After he deposits Lucynell at the convenient road stop, he gives no thought to his actions nor to Lucynell's precarious plight. He is somewhat depressed as he continues his journey, but he does not reflect on the cause of his despondency. After committing his shocking betrayal of the helpless halfwit in his charge, he picks up a hitchhiker because "he felt that a man with a car had a responsibility to others." After outrageously betraying the trust of the aged mother, who was manifestly devoted to her child, despite her many imperfections, he launches into a discourse on the merits of his own parent: "It's nothing so sweet . . . as a boy's mother. She taught him his first prayers at her knee, she give him love when no other would, she told him what was right and what wasn't, and she seen that he done the right thing. . . . My mother was a angel of Gawd."

The hitchhiker, disgusted with Mr. Shiftlet's sentimental display, retorts angrily, "you go to the devil" and leaps from the car.[10] Of course, Mr. Shiftlet has long since been of the devil's party. He assumes that it is the world which is corrupt and interprets his inner sense of decay as a reaction to "the rottenness of the world" which "was about to engulf him." As the storm clouds gather overhead, Mr. Shiftlet, in an amazing display of self-righteousness, calls upon his creator: " 'Oh Lord!' he prayed. 'Break forth and wash the slime from this earth!' " The mounting thunder and the huge raindrops, crashing "like tincan tops" on the roof of his car, suggest that he may not have to wait long before his prayers are answered. But Mr. Shiftlet has failed to heed the roadside warning: "Drive carefully. The life you save may be your own." Racing along the highway to Mobile, he does not notice that his own spiritual life is in imminent danger.[11]

IV   *Arrivals and Departures:*
"A Stroke of Good Fortune" and
"A Late Encounter with the Enemy"

The stories already discussed in this chapter are concerned with mystery and with violations of the sacramental view of life; they deal, respectively, with the mysteries of baptism, incarnation, and marriage. Two other stories—"A Stroke of Good Fortune" and "A Late Encounter with the Enemy"—are related to this group, concerned as they are with a distorted response to the two most basic human experiences, life and death. Birth becomes an occasion of despair instead of joy, and death occurs as a drama of pride instead of as an instruction in humility.

"A Stroke of Good Fortune" has, like most of O'Connor's stories, a highly ironic title. Ruby Hill, who has been assured by a fortune-teller that she will meet with good fortune, interprets the prophecy to mean that she will at last be able to move from her drab apartment dwelling into a new subdivision. She is horrified to discover that she is, instead, pregnant—a fate she has studiously avoided all her married life.

Ruby's abhorrence of motherhood reflects an attitude pervasive in the modern world. Basically, her view arises out of her own pride and selfishness. She is proud of her looks; proud of Bill Hill, her husband; and proud of her escape from the country to the city. In retrospect, she concludes that she was the only one of the eight children in her family "who had any git." Moreover, she selfishly wishes to preserve herself, for she remembers that these eight children had drained her mother's life—turned her into a "puckered-up old yellow apple"—at an early age. The mother had paid for each new life with something subtracted from her own: "Her mother had got deader with every one of them." Ruby recalls particularly the prolonged suffering her mother had undergone in giving birth to her baby brother Rufus, who had "turned out now to have no more charge than a dishrag." In all, the struggle to bear life seems a useless task; for, of the eight children, four had failed to reach maturity: "Two born dead, one died the first year, one crushed under a mowing machine." Ruby's two surviving sisters have failed to grasp the lesson implicit in their mother's futile maternity, for each has been married four years, and each has four children. Ruby concludes that their participation in the universal cycle of procreation is a result of nothing but "pure ignorance. The purest of downright ignorance."

We find in Ruby Hill's attitude a summation of the traditional arguments against childbearing: it destroys the health and beauty of the mother; a discouraging percentage of the offspring do not long survive; and those who do are of little worth or merit. Obviously, if all the world shared Ruby's selfish views, the race itself would come to an abrupt end and the problems of suffering and age would be solved, along with all other human problems. The life principle, however, is stronger than personal whim. It finds ways of asserting itself, subverting even the most sophisticated human programs to stifle its expression. Despite all Bill Hill's precautions, Ruby becomes pregnant, whether she likes it or not. She cannot escape her role as participant in the universal process of creation, for some things are of greater importance than moving into subdivisions and avoiding gray hair.

Ruby has steadfastly hardened her heart against all thoughts of motherhood. When she experiences a shortness of breath while climbing the stairs, she wonders not whether she is pregnant but if indeed she might have "heart trouble." (Mr. Jerger, the neighbor, avers that he has discovered the fountain of youth in his own heart.) Ruby Hill has, of course, been "dead" for many years. Her rejection of her natural role as parent serves to alienate her totally from the surging life forces of a universe which operates on a principle of constant self-renewal. Her lassitude is contrasted with the vitality of Laverne, a bouncy creature who sees romantic possibilities in Rufus, even though he is relatively young and ignorant. It is Laverne who reveals to Ruby the obvious cause of her ailment. Ruby, because of her unnatural terror of this natural development, has steadfastly ignored all the signs of pregnancy, and she also heatedly rejects Laverne's diagnosis. However, Madam Z has foreseen a "stroke of good fortune" in her future; and Hartley Gilfeet's mother specifically calls her own son "Little Mister Good Fortune." Sitting alone on the stairwell, Ruby pronounces the words that seem to indicate her future, and a leering echo answers "Good Fortune, Baby."

In many respects, this seems the weakest of the stories in *A*

Good Man Is Hard to Find. The issues are less pressing, and the characters are of less inherent interest. Moreover, "A Stroke of Good Fortune" is unusual in the O'Connor canon in that nothing of a truly catastrophic nature occurs. The fact that the basic movement is toward revelation rather than catastrophe serves to vitiate the ultimate impact. Perhaps the fact that this was the first published of the collected stories accounts for its comparative ineffectiveness.

Mr. Tom Shiftlet had posed the question, "What is a man?"; in "A Late Encounter with the Enemy" O'Connor presents various answers to the query. In this story, General Sash is considered from many points of view—his own, his family's, the public's. The portrait that finally emerges is one of the most effectively achieved comic creations in O'Connor's canon. The comedy arises out of the many ironies produced from the various cross-reflections in the story. The story has, of course, a tragic dimension as well; for General Sash's curiously realized death leads to sober reflection on the mystery which surrounds the end of life.

General Tennessee Flintrock Sash, though one hundred and four years old and confined to a wheelchair, is an exceedingly vain old man. Despite his advanced age and debilitated condition, General Sash is convinced that he is extremely handsome. He has agreed to appear onstage during his daughter's college graduation ceremony, not because he attributes any significance to the occasion itself, but because he welcomes the chance to appear in public: "When he put on his full-dress general's uniform, he knew well enough there was nothing to match him anywhere." The General obstinately refuses to wear teeth "because he thought his profile was more striking without them." In his stubborn pride and irascible temper, the General is related to the other fierce old men who appear so frequently in O'Connor's work. Mr. Head's absurd conceit, Mr. Fortune's destructive willfulness, even old Tarwater's radical contempt for the world around him are reflected in part in the character of General Sash, whose vanity governs his attitudes toward himself and the world. "Vanity" as such is a key concept in the story in the dual sense of an exaggerated self-esteem and of the uselessness of a life unrelated to any purpose outside itself.

To his daughter, Sally Poker Sash, the General is also a source of pride. Forced to attend the state teacher's college for the past

twenty summers to complete her degree, she is at last ready to
graduate at the age of sixty-two; she has prayed every night that
her father will last for the ceremony. The old man's presence on
stage will be public affirmation of her aristocratic heritage, proof
of "what all was behind her." It will also serve as a stinging re-
buke to those who have "turned the world on its head and unsettled the decent ways of living."

Sally, however, suffers occasional reminders that the legend
of the "glorious upright old man" has been considerably embel-
lished through the years. She is aware that the role he had played
in the Civil War was relatively insignificant (he had probably
been a foot-soldier). When the Hollywood crew had arrived in
Atlanta for the world premier of *Gone With the Wind,* she had
introduced her father by his true name (George Poker Sash) and
had elevated his rank only as far as Major. However, when she
arranges for her parent to sit onstage with the distinguished
visitors at her graduation, she informs the Dean that he was a
Confederate general and that his mind is still "clear as bell" (by
now he does not remember the war at all). Medically, the General is little more than a human vegetable: "His feet were completely dead now, his knees worked like old hinges, his kidneys
functioned when they would, but his heart persisted doggedly to
beat."

To her nephew, John Wesley Poker Sash, is delegated the task
of tending to the old gentleman on the ceremonial occasion. The
young Boy Scout is little concerned with his grandfather's celebrated status; to him, the old man is merely a piece of cumber-
some baggage to be parked hatless in the burning sun while he
(John Wesley) refreshes himself at the Coca-Cola machine.

To the faithful preservers of the Southern heritage, the old
man is a valuable relic out of a glorious past. Each year on Confederate Memorial Day, he is bundled up and lent to the Capitol
City Museum, where he is put on display along with the old
Civil War artillery and uniforms. During the spring, when the
plantation homes are opened for pilgrimage, he is often invited
to "sit in some conspicuous spot and lend atmosphere to the
scene."

The attitude toward General Sash of the various history-minded
groups suggests the transformations which history itself has undergone through the years. For the General, the past has faded

to a near-total blankness; in fact, as we have noted, he no longer remembers the war or his part in it, although his role as participant gives him such historic value to the present age. Onstage, hearing the speaker pronounce the names of Chickamauga and Lee, he wonders in which of these battles he had fought. The literal facts of history have likewise dimmed in the consciousness of this later generation. As the truth has receded, they have supplied from their own imaginations a colorful "recollection" of their glorious heritage. Thus, the old man is supplied with appropriate rank, name, and uniform for his reconstructed role. The vulgarization of the past by the glamour-minded present is epitomized in the Atlanta premiere, when usherettes in Confederate caps and short skirts held crossed Confederate and Union flags while the band played the "Battle Hymn of the Republic." This "preemy" is the single event that remains clearly in the old man's mind, primarily because of the attention he received from the many Hollywood starlets imported for the occasion. The total phoniness of the entire episode is epitomized in the "exquisite" corsage which the movie people presented to Sally Poker: it was made of "gladiola petals taken off and painted gold and put back together to look like a rose." The artificial flower perfectly reflects the synthetic view of history favored by some Southerners. They, like the old soldier, prefer parades to processions, the past revised into a Hollywood spectacular.

Sally is successful in getting her parent onstage for her own moment of academic triumph, but he does not last through the ceremony. The dying of General Sash is one of the most effectively handled scenes of expiration in O'Connor's work. Although the most significant episode in the old man's life occurs onstage, in full view of an audience, neither he nor the onlookers are aware of what is happening. The little hole which had appeared in the old man's head while he sat in the sun now begins to widen, and into it pours a confusion of sound, visual images, and memory. The words of the speaker handing out the diplomas come at him like musket fire. As the music swells,

> The entire past opened up on him out of nowhere and he felt his body riddled in a hundred places with sharp stabs of pain. . . . He saw his wife's narrow face looking at him critically through her round gold-rimmed glasses; he saw one of his squint-

ing bald-headed sons; and his mother ran toward him with an anxious look; then a succession of places—Chickamauga, Shiloh, Marthasville—rushed at him as if the past were the only future now and he had to endure it. Then suddenly he saw that the black procession was almost on him. He recognized it, for it had been dogging all his days. He made such a desperate effort to see over it and find out what comes after the past that his hand clenched the sword until the blade touched bone.

The demise of General Sash is remarkable in O'Connor's work, for it is one of her few presentations of death from "natural" causes. It shares with her other death scenes a bizarre quality that arises from her typical mixture of the comic and the macabre. Indeed, though from a medical point of view General Sash is obviously a victim of old age, we feel that, in some peculiar sense, he is at last struck down by the overweening pride in which he has so long indulged. His ending seems prepared by some cosmic jokester who arranges a fitting exit for the ancient, ego-ridden fraud. The absurd ending leads, finally, as in all her work, to a serious consideration of the fact of mortality as the inescapable feature of the human condition; and it draws the mind once again to Mr. Shiftlet's question, with its obvious tragic implications.

The question "What is a man?" can never be fully answered. The central episodes of a man's life can be viewed, but the mystery which outlines his career at every step can never be completely dispelled. Birth, baptism, matrimony, death—all, if properly understood, must be seen as stages in the ongoing scheme of redemption. For Flannery O'Connor, the many mysteries inherent in the fusion of human and divine, natural and sacramental, converge in the "central Christian mystery," the paradox that life "has, for all its horror, been found by God to be worth dying for."

CHAPTER 6

More Prophets Called:
The Violent Bear It Away and
"The Lame Shall Enter First"

THE central features of the novel *The Violent Bear It Away* [1]
show in both character and in action notable affinity with
those of *Wise Blood*. Young Tarwater, like Hazel, is the product
of a backwoods evangelistic tradition. Hazel's preacher grandfather imbued the boy with a fierce intention to serve the Lord,
and Tarwater's great-uncle, Mason Tarwater, who is also fired by
a messianic zeal, has trained the boy to follow in his steps. At
the beginning of the story, young Tarwater, like Hazel, has consciously rejected his destiny; he too is a fugitive from the Lord.
Each is in time brought to earth by the relentless hound of
heaven; and, in each story, the reversal of conscious intent is
effected through a series of violent acts, achieved in a threefold
pattern. Initially, the "fugitive" himself commits an act of violence: each performs a ritual murder to free himself for the events
to come. Next, each is subjected himself to a violation of person
or property. The final issue is an abrupt transformation of purpose, and the disciple is sealed through a dramatic act to the
service of his calling.

For Hazel, as we have seen, the pattern evolves as the killing
of the false prophet Solace Layfield, the destruction of his car by
the hostile patrolman, and the consummate act of self-blinding
as testimony to his dedication to the Holy Spirit. Tarwater drowns
his idiot cousin Bishop in the act of baptizing him, suffers rape
from the sinister stranger, and ends by setting the landscape
ablaze in an orgy of purification before setting forth to the city
to perform his prophetic mission. Though the basic pattern of
flight, apprehension, and capitulation is similar in each story, the

final outcome is different. Hazel chooses the course of expiation through self-mortification, thus withdrawing from the world of man into the realm of the spirit. Tarwater opts for the role of inspired preacher, the angry awakener of the sleeping city. Both Hazel and Tarwater are young men at war with God and themselves, but each clings to vestiges of his former identity, even while renouncing it. Tarwater, like Hazel, wears his hat at all times as a badge of his identity. Even after he seeks out his town uncle and is presumably ready to enter upon a new role, he stead-fastly refuses the new clothes which the uncle (Rayber) buys for him; he wears, instead, the clothes he had arrived in, overalls and old man's drawers. Hazel's clothes frequently cause him to be taken for a preacher.

On the road and in the city, both ex-prophets encounter the characteristic depravities of modern society. The sexual defile-ments offered by Sabbath Lily Hawks and Leora Watts are in-tensified in the act of the rapist who accosts Tarwater. The com-mercial rituals enacted by the potato-peeler salesman on the sidewalk and by Slade in the used car lot are elaborated by the copper flue salesman who gives Tarwater a ride and explains that "you couldn't sell a copper flue to a man you didn't love." The religious phoniness of Asa Hawks and Onnie Jay Holy in *Wise Blood* is repeated in the missionary family, which exploits its child evangelist as a profitable enterprise. The advice of the woman columnist who tells Lily Hawks to adjust to the modern world is expanded into a philosophy of life by the schoolteacher Rayber.

Thus, both Hazel and Tarwater, emerging from a world whose spiritual boundaries are rigidly defined by the stern morality of an ancient tradition, find themselves plunged into a world of sin as that quality is defined by their inherited tradition. Each tries in vain to adapt to the unfamiliar world in which evil constantly asserts itself, though all the while it insists that it (evil) no longer exists. Hazel throws in his lot with the devil by establishing his "Church Without Christ"; Tarwater, by studiedly avoiding the baptismal appointment made for him by his granduncle. Each, of course, is defeated; it is not the nature of grace easily to forgo those it has once touched.

The image of sight, the primary metaphor in *Wise Blood*, is also emphasized in *The Violent Bear It Away*. In *Wise Blood*, sight is equated with spiritual vision; the image is sustained through the absorbed scrutiny of Hazel's face by onlookers, by the final vision that precedes his blinding, and by the climactic act by which he renounces outward seeing for interior illumination. In *The Violent Bear It Away*, each character's eyes correspond to his inner spiritual state: the granduncle bears the fish-colored eyes of the prophet; Rayber, the mechanical man, peers forth from "small drill-like eyes set in the depths of twin glass caverns"; Bishop, who resembles old Tarwater in many ways, has eyes which are predictably blank, "clear, as if the other side of them went down and out into two pools of light"; the eyes of the devil, who pretends to be Tarwater's friend, are first hidden under a broad hat, but ultimately Tarwater sees that they are violet-colored, as are those of the rapist later. As for Tarwater himself, his eyes at first resemble those of his own father, the divinity student who had killed himself because of a sense of guilt; finally, when Tarwater has at last embraced his role of God's emissary, his eyes are those of the prophet, singed and "black in their deep sockets."

I *Torn by Hunger*

Though *The Violent Bear It Away* shares much in common with *Wise Blood*, it obviously has many features which are clearly distinguishable as its own. Eye imagery serves an important function in the story, but the primary image is that of the grandfather after death, who is sharing a meal of loaves and fishes with the blessed in heaven. Each repetition of "fish-colored" to describe the old man's eyes is a reminder of the biblical parable which is the unifying metaphor of the action. The old man proclaims repeatedly that "Jesus is the bread of life"; and the child, listening, trembles lest he too find himself some day "torn by hunger like the old man, the bottom split out of his stomach so that nothing would heal or fill it but the bread of life."

This concept of *spiritual hunger* is emphasized through many references to food on the literal level. When Rayber follows the boy out into the night, he observes the child pause thoughtfully before a store window. Hurrying forward to discover what has attracted the child's attention, Rayber finds that Tarwater has been staring into a bakery window which is empty except for a single loaf; the spiritual significance of the bread loaf in this scene is further heightened by the fact that the boy is on his way to a revivalist church meeting. During his stay with Rayber, Tarwater finds himself almost incapable of eating; when, on his journey home, the truck driver gives him a secondhand sandwich, the boy, though he is near starvation by this time, cannot force it down. He is gnawed by a vast hunger, one which can never be assuaged by physical sustenance.

In the boy's final vision at the farm, he sees his grandfather seated among the multitudes who are being fed from a single basket. At this point, the young prophet at last accepts his God-, appointed mission, for he is finally aware that the object of his hunger "was the same as the old man's and that nothing on earth would fill him. . . . He felt it rising in himself through time and darkness, rising through the centuries, and he knew that it rose in a line of men whose lives were chosen to sustain it, who would wander in the world, strangers from that violent country where the silence is never broken except to shout the truth." Thus, he moves toward the city like John the Baptist, who came from the wilderness "neither eating nor drinking."

Although both *Wise Blood* and *The Violent Bear It Away* share the figure of the aged prophet, the character of Old Tarwater is much more fully developed.[2] *Violent* opens on the day of the old man's death, but we get a very full picture of his prior life and background. We learn of his fanatic dedication to the fundamental tenets of sin, death, and resurrection through Christ. Like a true prophet, he sometimes disappeared into the back country for days at a time to thrash out his peace with the Lord. When he returned, he looked to the boy "as if he had been wrestling a wild cat, as if his head were still full of the visions he had seen in his eyes, wheels of light and strange beasts with giant wings of fire and four heads turned to the four points of the universe." At one point, Tarwater's sister had committed the aged fanatic to a mental institution, where he had remained for four years until he had discovered that the way to freedom lay in ceasing his attempts to convert the inmates. Later, he had cast himself upon the charity of his nephew in town, only to discover that the young scholar had made him an object of a case study, as a final specimen of "an ancient breed now all but extinct."

Flannery O'Connor's affinity with Hawthorne is here evident, for once more she offers us a "multiple choice" in interpretation

of character.[3] Hawthorne suggests in the *Scarlet Letter* many possibilities for Hester's true nature, from most debased of sinners
to most exalted of saints. Likewise, Tarwater can be seen in
various lights as a harmless relic of a lost age, as a madman, or
as a true prophet called of God. The fact that there is a strain
of madness in the family makes the distinctions even more difficult to draw. Old Tarwater is convinced of his own prophetic role;
when he steals the infant Tarwater, he leaves Rayber the warning:
"THE PROPHET I RAISE UP OUT OF THIS BOY WILL BURN YOUR EYES
CLEAN." He gives the boy an education suited to his future calling:
"His uncle had taught him Figures, Reading, Writing, and History beginning with Adam expelled from the Garden and going
on down through the presidents to Herbert Hoover and on in
speculation toward the Second Coming and the Day of Judgment."

Rayber, the schoolteacher, though subjected briefly in his youth
to the old man's indoctrinations, has long since rejected the outworn creed, on a rational level. Rayber has thrown in his lot
with modern psychological theories which reject the ancient law
and substitute subconscious motives for spiritual drives. In his
published study of his uncle, Rayber explained that the old man,
to relieve his own sense of insecurity, had simply "called" himself
to his holy career. Moreover, Rayber is committed to "testing" as a
way of uncovering the essential truth of human character. He
is in charge of his school's testing program, and he is particularly
unsettled by his young nephew's refusal to submit to standard
measurement procedures. Rayber's electric hearing aid emphasizes
his abdication of the human for the mechanical approach; he is,
indeed, "a man trapped in a switch box."

The old man is outraged when he discovers the use which his
nephew has made of him: "Where he wanted me was inside that
schoolteacher magazine. He thought once he got me in there,
I'd be as good as inside his head and done for and that would
be that, that would be the end of it." Rayber is guilty of the sin
which so concerned Hawthorne, the violation of the human
heart. He is like Chillingworth, who scrutinizes Dimmesdale with
the detachment of a scientist coldly examining a specimen, or
Ethan Brand, who roams the world observing mankind with detachment in his inhuman search for the "unforgivable sin." But
Rayber never comes to a recognition of his own transgression.

Blinded by his futile reliance on collected data as an approach to truth, he has lost the sense of oneness with humanity, the awareness of mankind bound together in the sacred family of God. As O'Connor has explained, "I wanted to get across the fact that the great Uncle (Old Tarwater) is the Christian—a sort of crypto-Catholic—and that the school teacher (Rayber) is the typical modern man. The boy (young Tarwater) has to choose which one, which way, he wants to follow. It's a matter of vocation." [4]

Rayber, however, does not totally succeed in his attempted rejection of his spiritual legacy. Intellectually, he embraces atheism; but emotionally he is still susceptible to the secret urgings of the spirit toward the holy embrace. He lives a highly guarded life, carefully steering a narrow course between "madness" and "nothing"—but he is ready to fall toward nothingness if the need arises. He knows that the seed planted in him by his uncle can, though withered, be brought to life again. Rayber is especially perturbed by his uncontrollable love for his child Bishop, an emotion which rises up in him from time to time with an ungovernable force. Bishop, fated to remain always mentally at the five-year-old level, is, Rayber insists, a mistake of nature—an irrefutable argument against the existence of a benevolent deity.[5] Yet, clearly, Rayber's deep affection for the idiot boy, inexplicable in terms of logic, implies a corresponding love of God for his creation, including its malformed and deficient members as well as those who are normal and whole.

The presence of the defective child again introduces at the heart of the story an abiding theological paradox. The problem of reconciling God's mercy with the spectacle of the damaged creature is one which has long occupied the attention of both attackers against, and defenders of, a system of cosmic justice. God's detractors insist that the defective being is undeniable proof that ours is a godless universe, or it is one powered by forces indifferent or hostile to man's welfare. The opposition insists that these apparent deviations from the divine scheme are but mysterious fragments in an inscrutable design whose ultimate purpose will be accounted for once the scheme is revealed in totality. As we have noted, this central mystery is obviously one which strongly attracted Flannery O'Connor throughout her life. She attacks the problem directly in "A Temple of the Holy Ghost," where the hermaphrodite at the fair awakens in the young child deep reflections on God's purpose and intent.

The variously malformed creatures in O'Connor's work, the physical grotesques and the spiritually misshapen, remind us again and again that we live in a fallen universe, that the ideal concept seldom finds its perfect embodiment in the physical actuality. Furthermore, the obviously deformed call attention to themselves as oddities within the human family, yet they manifest in actuality merely exaggerations or extensions of the imperfections that mark all God's creatures. O'Connor seems to ask by implication: if God rejects the retarded Bishop or the circus freak, why should he love us? If truth were known, our hidden infirmities differ only in the slightest degree from their revealed deficiencies.

To old Tarwater, the mentally defective Bishop cannot be dismissed as merely a "freak of nature." He is God's own child, a soul in need of baptismal purification to guarantee his eligibility for salvation. The central action of the story focuses on the attempt to redeem Bishop through the sacrament of baptism. Having failed in his own persistent efforts to baptize Bishop, old Tarwater lays the sacred charge upon his chosen heir, young Tarwater, whose successful achievement of the act will serve a twofold purpose: the salvation of the child and the confirmation of young Tarwater in his role as prophet. As the devil correctly warns Tarwater, "If you baptize once, you'll be doing it the rest of your life."

II A Dying into Life

In Christian doctrine, baptism is a key rite in the progress toward salvation. The recognition of Christ's role as the Redeemer is thus achieved; and, through that recognition, man is accepted into the kingdom of the saved. The act itself is the necessary commemoration of the "dying into life," the renunciation of the fleshly self and the embracing of the spiritual identity. Through the baptism, the believer confirms his acceptance of "Christ crucified" and of the sacrificial atonement thereby achieved. The baptismal sacrament is thus of paramount significance to all versions of Christian faith, from Protestant fundamentalism to Catholicism.

The emphasis on this central rite as essential to salvation is seen throughout the story in reference to the baptisms of the various characters. Old Tarwater—through stealth, cunning, and courage—had succeeded in performing the rites for Rayber and young Tarwater, even though the act for Rayber involved a kidnapping and for young Tarwater the employment of the water from the baby's own bottle. All Tarwater's efforts to "save" Bishop have been futile because of Rayber's opposition, and hence he lays this task upon his grandnephew as his elected successor.

Young Tarwater's successful execution of the baptismal mission marks the beginning of his acceptance of his role as prophet, but it also raises a major paradox of the story: the enigma of salvation by drowning.[6] The drowning of Bishop is itself a literal realization of the symbolic significance of the ritual: baptism symbolizes the death of the old self so that a new self may be born. Many fundamentalists insist that the ceremony should as nearly as possible reproduce the conditions of an actual "drowning." The subject is fully immersed in a river, lake, or baptistery as the holy words are repeated over him. Young Tarwater, of course, initially intends to kill, not to save, the child. But at the crucial moment he involuntarily repeats the ritual formulas, and thus the event is for Bishop a salvation as well as an annihilation.

The fact that Tarwater does commit a murder, even though it occurs in the act of baptism, is a moral point difficult to resolve within the religious frame of the story. It can, of course, be said that the effect is somewhat diminished by Bishop's state as a mental defective. In addition, Tarwater's own youthful innocence serves to relieve him somewhat of culpability. The whole affair suggests a ritual killing, whose ethical implications are outweighed by what is thereby attained in the growth of young Tarwater's character. Now he embraces his inexorable destiny; the act is irrevocable, and he himself can escape with nothing less than a full commitment. The dramatic end of Bishop also refutes Rayber's claim that "Nothing ever happens to that kind of child," and it reinforces young Tarwater's boast that he can "make something happen." It reminds us of the violence suggested by the title of the story, and it recalls that the young Tarwater hails from a place called Powderhead.

III *Further Emblems of Death and Regeneration*

Water, then, is employed as a basic symbol of death and spiritual rebirth. Other symbols also are employed in similar dual significance. In fact, in this novel O'Connor, like Eliot in *The Waste Land*, utilizes each of the four primary elements as an emblem of death and regeneration. The role of the earth as redemptive symbol is seen through the action which deals with the burial of Old Tarwater's body. The old man himself is so deeply concerned that his body be buried intact and not be subjected to some pagan rite of cremation, that he has prepared his own coffin and has given his grandnephew specific instructions as to how the act of burial is to be achieved. Believing in the literal resurrection of the body at the day of judgment, the elderly preacher insists that he be interred in a proper grave, one marked with the cross so that he can be correctly identified when the faithful are called on resurrection day. Young Tarwater disobeys his uncle's command by setting fire to the house with the corpse inside to indicate his sympathies with Rayber's atheistic position, but old Tarwater's wish is realized by his faithful Negro friend who places the body in the ground and marks the place with a crude cross.

When young Tarwater returns to Powderhead, he discovers the fresh grave-mound and realizes that the old man has triumphed in respect to his last wish as in everything else. When he hears the heavenly voice warning him to "GO WARN THE CHILDREN OF GOD OF THE TERRIBLE SPEED OF MERCY," it is as if the old prophet himself were speaking; for at this moment Tarwater has thrown himself upon the grave. Before he leaves his home for the last time, Tarwater marks his own forehead with earth from the new grave; this act indicates a sharing of the old man's identity (a token tribute to the prophet in death) and an acceptance of the prophetic role cast upon him. The act also signifies a final coming of age for young Tarwater; it suggests parallels with Isaac's initiation into the cult of the hunter in Faulkner's *The Bear:* Isaac, too, is marked with a ritual substance (blood) on his forehead. The earth token is also reminiscent of the service of Ash Wednesday, when ashes are placed on the foreheads of the faithful to remind them of death and of the sorrow they should feel for their sins.

Air, the third element, plays a less significant role as an emblem of redemption, but it does appear in a symbolic function at certain points. In the car of the rapist, young Tarwater feels almost suffocated by the strangely perfumed atmosphere. The cloying sweetness suggests the aura of moral corruption which surrounds the vampirish driver.[7] When the boy at last reaches the farm, the soft-voiced stranger is still whispering to him: "The presence was as pervasive as an odor, a warm sweet body of air encircling him, a violent shadow hanging around his shoulders." Tarwater's furious setting fire to the place where the rape occurs is a forceful act of ritual purification of the atmosphere.

The final element, fire, plays a role second in significance only to that of water. Fire is used primarily in its archetypal association with heavenly energy, an instrument of inspiration and purification. Old Tarwater, in preparation for his life mission, "had been burned clean and burned clean again. He had learned by fire." When he steals the child who is to be his spiritual heir, he leaves a warning for the teacher: "THE PROPHET I RAISE UP OUT OF THIS BOY WILL BURN YOUR EYES CLEAN." The child evangelist in town proclaims, "I've seen the Lord in a tree of fire! The Word of God is a burning Word to burn you clean!"

Three times young Tarwater sets fire to his surroundings, and each action is a highly significant one. The first—the burning of the house with the body of the uncle inside—is the boy's symbolic rejection of the spiritual legacy willed by his uncle. The second—the firing of the grove where the stranger has assaulted him—is a ritual of purification and a step toward the acceptance of his destiny, which now forces him on "to a final revelation." His eyes, from this point on, are as if seared by the holy flame. "His scorched eyes no longer looked hollow or as if they were meant only to guide him forward. They looked as if, touched with a coal like the lips of the prophet, they would never be used for ordinary sights again." In his third act of arson, he seeks to destroy the devil himself.

IV *A Devil Rejected and a Calling Embraced*

After Tarwater's ritual burning of the grove, he is still not totally committed to the destiny set before him. The mysterious voice which has whispered in his ear since the beginning of his experience speaks again, urging him on to a false position. The voice he hears is that of the devil, and the devil plays many roles in the story.[8] He appears as Meeks, the copper flue salesman, who insists that love of the customer is essential to salesmanship; as the stranger in the park, who urges "Be like me . . . don't let no jackasses tell you what to do"; and as the lavender-shirted driver who refreshes himself on the blood of the unsuspecting boy.

Most often, the devil visits the boy's consciousness as a disembodied voice, whispering, arguing, cajoling to lure him away from his heavenly vision and enlist him in his own demonic legions. The devil's insidious arguments rely on the usual formulas intended to tempt souls away from God: he argues that the notion of resurrection contradicts the facts of chemistry, that the old man was no prophet but a madman who wrote off the rest of the world as "whores and asses" and brought up the boy for the sole purpose of seeing that he himself got a proper burial. He also implants in the boy's mind a suspicion of all the old man has taught him: "How do you know that two added to two makes four? . . . How do you know if there was an Adam or if Jesus eased your situation any when he redeemed you?" Moreover, he taunts the boy with his failure to receive from God a sign to confirm his election as prophet; and he asserts that there is, in fact, no devil at all—that the real choice is between "Jesus and you."[9]

During young Tarwater's stay in town, he has numerous opportunities to baptize Bishop; but the devil always holds him back, urging that he has not yet received a proper sign. Tarwater's growing hunger is, he insists, merely a sensation, not a call from the Lord. During the tense episode in the park, when Tarwater almost realizes his purpose to baptize the child, the stranger (the devil in disguise) is at first silent "as if in the felt presence, he dare not raise his voice." When Tarwater fails of his intention, the voice accuses the boy of confusing a "madness with a mission." He further insists "The Lord is not studying about you, don't know you exist, and wouldn't do a thing about it if He did." Later, when Tarwater hesitates in the boat with Bishop, the voice urges him on, hissing: "It's only one dimwit you have to drown."

The driver who gives Tarwater a ride in his lavender- and cream-colored car is identified as the devil by unmistakable signs. The details of his appearance (the violet eyes and panama hat) match the earlier description of Tarwater's "friend." Tarwater himself detects "something familiar" about the stranger, but he is not sure what it is. His granduncle has specifically warned him to beware the devil's overtures: "You are the kind of boy . . . that the devil is always going to be offering to assist, to give you a smoke or a drink or a ride, and to ask you your bidnis." In the seduction scene, the devil, dressed in a lavender shirt, proceeds exactly as the old man had warned.[10] The boy, puffing the unfamiliar cigarette and swilling the searing liquor, assumes he is discrediting "all his greatuncle's warnings about poisonous liquor, all his idiot restrictions about riding with strangers."

When Tarwater finally makes his way to the charred homestead, the voice of his familiar friend (who has now been restored to invisibility) accompanies him. Looking on the seared landscape, Tarwater recognizes it as the sign of the broken covenant. His persistent friend whispers to him to "go down and take it. . . . It's ours. We've won it." At this moment, Tarwater at last resolves the dilemma which has torn his spirit so long. Seizing a pine bough, he sets the forest ablaze until there is "a rising wall of fire between him and the grinning presence. He glared through the flame and saw that his adversary would soon be consumed in a roaring blaze."

At this moment, when Tarwater so violently rejects the devil and his spiritual temptations, he at last receives the sign he has so long awaited. First, he discovers that his granduncle's corpse has not been consumed by fire, but has been given proper burial by Buford, with a cross at its head. Next, the boy has a great vision of the heavenly throngs feeding on the blessed loaves and fishes, with his granduncle in their midst. Turning to the treeline, Tarwater sees a tree blazing in red gold flame; he knows that "this was the fire that encircled Daniel, that had raised Elijah from the earth, that had spoken to Moses and would in the instant speak to him."

The call comes, unmistakable and clear; by midnight, he is on his way to town, purged by the holy flames of love. He is now, in a literal sense, the prophet out of the wilderness, as he moves "toward the dark city, where the children of God lay sleeping." Through violence, Tarwater has been restored to God; through his violent message, he will rouse the sleeping children to remembrance of their forgotten heavenly heritage.

V   A Journey into Space:
"The Lame Shall Enter First"

"The Lame Shall Enter First" is an obvious reworking of
The Violent Bear It Away, although the outcome differs significantly. Again, the central characters consist of a trio of father,
actual son, and surrogate son. Rayber of the novel and Sheppard
of the story are alike in that each seeks the "good" through active participation in a humanistic philanthropy. Sheppard, a city
recreational director, promotes social improvement by minister-
ing to his flock of Little Leaguers; in addition, he devotes his
Saturdays to a free counseling service at the reformatory. Like
Rayber, he is a convert to quantitative measurement as a way of
assessing human value. Hence, he is awed by his discovery that
Rufus Johnson, a young delinquent, scored at genius level on
an intelligence test. Like Rayber, Sheppard rejects all religious
dogma as the outworn relic of an unenlightened age. In the lib-
erated consciousness of the modern era, notions of good and evil
or of sin and retribution find no place. Sheppard seeks to trans-
form through action dissociated from belief. His society accepts
him as a "good" man, but Rufus bitterly rejects Sheppard's example: "I don't care if he's good or not. He ain't right!" In fact,
Rufus accuses Sheppard of confusing himself with Christ.

Norton, Sheppard's son, is, like Bishop, a disappointment to his
father: Norton is a moral rather than a mental defective. His
most conspicuous flaws are gluttony and avarice. He gorges himself until he vomits, suggesting the gluttons of Dante's third
circle, who exist embedded in the filth that is the product of their
vice. Norton, who sells seeds, lovingly fondles his profits daily;
and Sheppard foresees for his son a dire future as a banker or
as a small-loans agent. Sheppard hopes that the introduction of
another boy (Rufus) into the household will serve as a moral
corrective for his own son by teaching him "to share."

As an active delinquent, Rufus has moved one step nearer to
the devil's service than had young Tarwater. Rufus accounts for
his antisocial behavior with the staunch assertion that he is in the
power of Satan. But Rufus, like Tarwater, suffers an insistent
pull toward salvation. Unable to resist God's signals completely,
he steals a Bible in order to instruct Norton in its undeniable

truths; and, when Sheppard challenges his convictions, Rufus literally devours the holy pages as testimony to his belief.

Rufus's club foot is a key characteristic of his nature and a prime motif in the story. Sheppard, of course, seizes upon the foot as the unquestionable source of Rufus's delinquency, interpreting his criminal behavior as simple "compensation" for his physical defect. Rufus rejects both Sheppard's explanation and his offers of help: he senses that his refusal of the corrective shoe will be an ultimate revenge upon Sheppard for the latter's unwelcome generosity. The point here is that the gift of a new shoe will not cure the ailing Rufus since his moral deficiency derives from his alienation from God: not until he is "saved" in his own terms can he be healed and brought into a correct relationship with himself and his fellow men.

The action of *The Violent Bear It Away* centered on the imposed task of baptizing the halfwit son. In the shorter narrative, the action once again turns on the bringing of a child into contact with his spiritual heritage. Rufus acts as a divine agent even though he himself is admittedly of the devil's clan. Here once again is evidence of O'Connor's belief that active commitment to recognized evil is preferable to neutral uninvolvement.

The key symbol of the work is that of the stars, which are explored in the dual implication of the spiritual and physical heavens. For Sheppard, the stars as physical entities are to be explored through physical means, by a telescope in the attic or by a journey into space. For Rufus, heaven denotes the spiritual realm, a locale to be reached not in a spaceship but through the sustained efforts of a life committed to a transcendent ideal. Norton, who confuses the two views in his mind, accepts Rufus's declaration that his mother has gone to heaven, and he searches for her with his telescope until he locates her. He then hangs himself in order to join her, for Rufus has assured him that, if he dies now, he will indeed go to heaven, but that if he lives long enough, he will be corrupted and go to hell. Norton's extreme action is evidence of his acute longing for love. O'Connor's further implication is that, through Rufus's instructions, the boy *will* go to heaven. Had he lived out his life under the corrupt tutelage of his father, he *would* have been destined for hell.

Too late, Sheppard discovers that in his efforts to reform the intractible Rufus, he has fatally neglected his own son. His ethical relativism proves too weak a support for the actual demands of experience. One child imprisoned, one dead, Sheppard is left with only his Little League games and his Saturday sessions at the reformatory to console him for his losses. Here, once again, is Flannery O'Connor's stern indictment of a society which locates its values within a strictly human matrix. Without God, man drifts into seeming moral vacuums where the devil, in fact, is in control. Sheppard views himself as the redeeming priest of the modern world (his office at the reformatory resembles a confessional); Sheppard, however, does not absolve but "explains" human action. In truth, as Rufus sneeringly accuses, Sheppard is an unwitting servant of the devil. Rufus recognizes that the choice is clearly one of either-or: either he (Rufus) will continue his life of sin, realized through crimes that will ultimately deliver him to hell, or he will renounce his satanic role and become a preacher. There is no in-between, as Sheppard, with his "immoral suggestions" of atheism, learns to his irreparable sorrow.

CHAPTER 7

Stories of Grace and Revelation

THE problem of grace and redemption is one of constant concern to Flannery O'Connor. Human action is consistently set against a backdrop of metaphysical considerations. Actions of good or evil played out on the human stage echo the cosmic encounter between the forces of light and darkness. God wars with the devil for the human soul in the ancient clash.

The choice is clear. As the Misfit warns, "Jesus was the only one ever raised the dead. . . . If he did what He said, then it's nothing for you to do but thow away everything and follow him, and if He didn't, then it's nothing for you to do but enjoy the few minutes you got left the best way you can—by killing somebody or burning down his house or doing some other meanness to him." The Reverend Bevel Summers exhorts his audience to "Believe Jesus or the devil! . . . testify to one or the other!" Hazel Motes, having renounced his faith, establishes the Church Without Christ "where the blind don't see and the lame don't walk and what's dead stays that way . . . the church that the blood of Jesus don't foul with redemption."

There is no halfway point, for the soul must "testify to one or the other." We see numerous instances of those who have clearly consummated the devil's pact: Mr. Paradise, who renounces the preacher's message, manifests an extreme depravity in his pursuit of the innocent child; Mr. Shiftlet victimizes the hapless Lucynell in a clever con game; the enraged black actor in "Judgement Day" stuffs the helpless old man between the stairway bannisters of the New York apartment house and leaves him dangling there for his daughter to find.

Even those who consider themselves "good" are capable of gravest sins: Mrs. McIntyre rejects the priest's message and finds herself a participant in a communal murder; Mrs. Cope fastens on her property as her highest possession and must be instructed in humility. Basically, the "sinners" fall into two categories: the aggressively evil, who commit overt acts against person, property, or spirit; and the victims of pride, who live oblivious to their spiritual vanities until these are revealed through episodes of violence and trauma. The vain, ludicrous in their groundless sense of superiority, are like Mr. Head, who considers himself a worthy guide for the young, but cannot find his way around the city streets, or General Sash, who refuses to wear his false teeth because he considers himself handsomer without them. They are epitomized in the character of Mrs. Hopewell, who is gratified by the fact that she has "no bad qualities of her own."

Despite the abundant evidence of evil manifest in corrupt actions and in complacent attitudes, there is ample testimony to the workings of the counterforce of good on the human spirit. Young Tarwater is ravenous for the bread of life; he fears his hunger, for he knows it is finally unassuageable. The impostor Asa Hawks senses at once that "some preacher has left his mark" on Hazel Motes. Mankind is drawn to God, like the child who calls himself "Bevel" after the rural preacher, or like Rufus, who knows he is in Satan's power, but goes shoplifting for the Scriptures and devours its pages to prove his faith.

Revelation occurs in unforeseen moments, and grace descends in unexpected ways. Sometimes, the action of "grace" occurs within a context seemingly "natural" in its external features. Mrs. Cope's smug expression finally alters as she views the fire raging wildly in her woods. Julian ("Everything That Rises Must Converge"), running for help for his dying mother, is drawn inevitably toward "the world of guilt and sorrow." At other times, the Holy Spirit manifests itself in forms unquestionably "supernatural." The "miraculous" nature of the visitation is as undeniable as that of the bush burning in the desert or the water bursting from stone. Mr. Head, in "The Artificial Nigger," recognizes that his reconciliation with Nelson in the city occurs "like an action of mercy." At their homecoming, he again is moved by a sense of the divine spirit descending:

> Mr. Head stood very still and felt the action of mercy touch him again but this time he knew that there were no words in the world that could name it. He understood that it grew out of agony, which is not denied to any man and which is given in

strange ways to children. He understood it was all a man could carry into death to give his Maker and he suddenly burned with shame that he had so little of it to take with him. He stood appalled, judging himself with the thoroughness of God, while the action of mercy covered his pride like a flame and consumed it.

Through the miraculous agency of divine mercy, Mr. Head is reconciled—to God and to the unfortunate grandson he has so ignobly betrayed.

I   *A Purifying Terror*

Three stories in the second collection, *Everything That Rises Must Converge,* are specifically occupied with the operation of revelation and grace upon the human spirit through "suprahuman" manifestations: Asbury Fox in "The Enduring Chill" waits in terror as the Paraclete made visible descends upon his unwilling spirit; Mrs. Turpin in "Revelation" is at last shaken from pride when the sky literally opens above her to reveal her lowly position in the heavenly procession; O. E. Parker in "Parker's Back" is blinded by a fiery vision which drives him to accept at last the calling he has so long evaded.

In "The Enduring Chill," the imminence of death prepares Asbury for the descent of the Holy Ghost. Asbury, returned from New York City to wait extinction in the provinces, desperately yearns to undergo one significant experience before his life ends. He first seeks intellectual communion with a local priest, but the attempt fails when the cleric proves to be hopelessly uninformed about esthetic and cultural topics. Asbury next tries to arrange a last meeting with the black laborers on his mother's farm, in an attempt to re-create an earlier occasion when, smoking with the blacks in the barn, Asbury had felt racial differences dissolve in a moment of close communion. His efforts are futile, for the helpers, who do not understand Asbury's motives, leave amidst embarrassed confusion on their part and exasperation on his. Thus, the two experiences on which much of modern society relies to give "meaning" to its existence—sophisticated intellectual exchange and interracial involvement—prove worthless to Asbury in his need.

At last, the country doctor succeeds in diagnosing Asbury's illness; and he is informed that his malady, though serious, will not be fatal. It is then that he finally captures the sense of meaning which he had so desperately sought, but the terms are vastly different from those he had expected:

> It was then that he felt the beginning of a chill, a chill so peculiar, so light, that it was like a warm ripple across a deeper sea of cold. His breath came short. The fierce bird which through the years of his childhood and the days of his illness had been poised over his head, waiting mysteriously, appeared all at once to be in motion. Asbury blanched and the last film of illusion was torn as if by a whirlwind from his eyes. He saw that for the rest of his days, frail, racked, but enduring, he would live in the face of a purifying terror. A feeble cry, a last impossible protest escaped him. But the Holy Ghost, emblazoned in ice instead of fire, continued, implacable, to descend.

The "enduring terror" which Asbury's fate prepares for him arises out of his tardily awakened sense of his own insufficiency. He was prepared to die supported by a firm sense of his own superiority to the world he had already rejected. He is unprepared for a "life sentence" to a world in which he must daily confront the evidence of his own essential inadequacy.

II A Wart Hog from Hell: "Revelation"

"Revelation" is the story of the overthrow of pride, the presentation of a violent outward assault that leads to a deep inner illumination of self and to an adjustment of the sense of the self's relation to others. Mrs. Turpin, smug in her bland conviction of personal superiority, confidently places herself near the top of the social and spiritual hierarchy. A "good" woman, a worker in the church whose announced philosophy of life is to help those less fortunate; she also considers herself attractive physically, though she weighs one hundred and eighty-five pounds and is well into her forties. Above all, she prides herself on her good disposition, an attribute she considers essential to personal success. She constantly gives thanks to Jesus for his generosity in creating her as *herself* rather than as some less fortunate being.

Mrs. Turpin's gratifying sense of her own sufficiency leads her to reflect constantly on the inferior state of most of her fellow creatures. In the doctor's waiting room is assembled a diverse group, forming together a microcosm of society at large. Most of the types are easily classified by Mrs. Turpin: a pleasant older lady is clearly of "good blood" because she is well dressed and has an amiable expression; the lady's daughter is a puzzle, because, although she obviously comes from good stock, she glares hostilely from behind her book at Mrs. Turpin, even though they are so obviously of the same class; and the white-trash woman is easily identifiable by her snuff-stained lips and dirty child.

On entering the waiting room, Mrs. Turpin (Turnip?) at once strikes up a conversation with the other "lady" present, and they explore together the fascinations of Mrs. Turpin's weight problem, the Negro question, and the details of farm management. Mrs. Turpin's contributions to the dialogue are obviously well rehearsed. The door to her mind has long ago swung shut, and no approach short of violence can lead to any revision of her stubbornly held views.

In the conversation, Mrs. Turpin always concentrates attention on herself, the focal point of the world, and obviously the only topic of any real interest or importance. When her companion asks Claud, her husband, the nature of his illness, Mrs. Turpin promptly answers, "A cow kicked him." Her husband, then, is merely her satellite, an extension of her own personality.

Mrs. Turpin's continuing pleasure in her own identity is sometimes challenged by the thought that she might have been assigned to some other role on earth:

> Sometimes at night when she couldn't go to sleep, Mrs. Turpin would occupy herself with the question of who she would have chosen to be if she couldn't have been herself. If Jesus had said to her before he made her, "There's only two places available for you. You can either be a nigger or white 'trash,'" what would she have said? "Please, Jesus, please," she would have said, "just let me wait until there's another place available," and he would have said, "No, you have to go right now and I have only those two places so make up your mind." She would have wiggled and squirmed and begged and pleaded but it would have been no use and finally she would have said, "All right, make me a nigger then—but that don't mean a trashy one." And he would

have made her a neat clean respectable Negro woman, herself but black.

Mrs. Turpin lives by a rigidly constructed view of the social hierarchy: "Sometimes Mrs. Turpin occupied herself at night naming the classes of people. On the bottom of the heap were most colored people, not the kind she would have been if she had been one, but most of them; then next to them—not above, just away from—were the white-trash; then above them were the home-owners, and above them the home-and-land owners, to which she and Claud belonged. Above she and Claud were people with a lot of money and much bigger houses and much more land."

At this point, however, complexities arise to challenge the neat compartmentalization: "But here the complexity of it would begin to bear in on her, for some of the people with a lot of money were common and ought to be below she and Claud and some of the people who had good blood had lost their money and had to rent and then there were colored people who owned their homes and land as well."

Mrs. Turpin is thus a person with fixed views of herself and the universe, who carries an assured sense of her own superior position with respect to the rest of the human race. Finally, she can contain her jubilation for her own state of blessedness no longer. She cries aloud to her unsuspecting audience, "Oh thank you, Jesus, Jesus, thank you!" In her words we hear a distinct echo of the Pharisee's prayer, "God, I thank thee, that I am not as other men are . . ." (Luke 18:11).

The destruction of Mrs. Turpin's smug assumptions of superiority occurs in a violent and unexpected form. The young girl in the office who has glared at Mrs. Turpin persistently during Mrs. Turpin's exchange of remarks with those around her is roused to action by the latter's outburst. In frenzied rage, she flings her book at Mrs. Turpin and physically assaults her. When Mrs. Turpin asks, "What you got to say to me?," the girl answers, "Go back to hell where you came from, you old wart hog." [1]

This is the first revelation, the sudden opening up of a possible character for Mrs. Turpin totally antithetic to her self-image. She fails to absorb the full meaning of the message at once, but the ultimate consequence is a total revision of her picture of the

orders of creation. The immediate effect of the physical attack
had been a dislocation of her normal visual perception: at first,
everything seemed to her small and far away, as if she were looking through the wrong end of a telescope; then everything re-
versed, becoming very large and close.[2] The result of the psychological assault is, likewise, a significantly changed inner perspective. Mrs. Turpin, who prides herself on her good disposition,
becomes strangely glum; she is even resentful of the doctor's
attempts to aid her. As she and Claud return home, she half expects to find that their house has been destroyed in their absence. Having discovered her vulnerability to catastrophe, she
feels that anything is liable to happen.

The initial revelation—the ugly insult hurled at Mrs. Turpin
by the rude young girl—is followed by a second: her own account
of her mistreatment to the black laborers who have come in from
the field. Although the blacks respond in tones of lavish sympathy, she is left uncomforted. She realizes that the blacks—unlike the Wellesley girl in the doctor's office—are dutifully saying
what they know they are expected to say. The scene in which
Mrs. Turpin vainly seeks consolation from the black field hands
effectively epitomizes the impossibility of real communication
between the races (given the rigidity of the Southern social hierarchy), and also suggests the comic irony implicit in the situation
where the white suffers from circumstances which he himself
has created.

Still unconsoled, Mrs. Turpin proceeds to the pigpen, to confront directly her unseen accuser. Here, she engages in a wrathful
dialogue with God, protesting the injustice of the indictment
levied against her:

> "What do you send me a message like that for?" she said in a
> low fierce voice, barely above a whisper but with the force of a
> shout in its concentrated fury. "How am I a hog and me both?
> How am I saved and from hell too?" . . .

> "I could quit working and take it easy and be filthy," she
> growled. "Lounge about the sidewalks all day drinking root beer.
> Dip snuff and spit in every puddle and have it all over my
> face. I could be nasty."

In a final surge of fury, she challenges God: "Who do you think you are?" "The question carried over the pasture and across the highway and the cotton fields and return to her clearly like an answer from beyond the wood." In other words, Mrs. Turpin is at last forced to confront the question of her own self-identity. In the sudden disintegration of her world view, Mrs. Turpin is introduced to an image of reality directly antithetic to all that she has hitherto maintained. Although still apparently unpersuaded on the rational plane, Mrs. Turpin succumbs on a far deeper level. "Sometimes," says Evelyn Underhill, "mystical intuition takes the form of a sudden and ungovernable uprush of knowledge from the depths of personality." [3] This "sudden and ungovernable uprush of knowledge" expresses itself now in a dramatic vision in which Mrs. Turpin receives vivid evidence of the errors of her ways:

> She saw the streak as a vast swinging bridge extending upward from the earth through a field of living fire. Upon it a vast horde of souls were rumbling toward heaven. There were whole companies of white-trash, clean for the first time in their lives, and bands of black niggers in white robes, and battalions of freaks and lunatics shouting and clapping and leaping like frogs. And bringing up the end of the procession was a tribe of people whom she recognized at once as those who, like herself and Claud, had always had a little of everything and the God-given wit to use it right. . . . she could see by their shocked and altered faces that even their virtues were being burned away.

Mrs. Turpin is first exposed to violent physical and spiritual attack; such ferocity of assault was obviously necessary to unbend her proud spirit. The revelation that comes to her at last is confirmation of her own insignificance in the spiritual order. She is literally blasted out of her moral sloth into a new awareness of self. At last, she discovers the virtue of humility.

III   A Byzantine Christ: "Parker's Back"

O. E. Parker, like Jonah, Saint Francis, and Hazel Motes, is a man who tries in vain to flee the hound of heaven. The name his mother gave to him, Obadiah Elihu,[4] suggests his inescapable destiny as a child of God, but he steadfastly rejects the possibility of salvation and shortens his name to noncommital initials. Against his will and for reasons he himself does not understand, he is drawn to a gaunt woman who is stern in her devotion to the Lord, and he ultimately finds himself married to her. Parker's wife is in every way the opposite of himself: her unpainted lips contrast with his brightly adorned body; her reverential invoking of the holy name, with his promiscuous cursing; her primly puritan views, with his "sexy" approach to life. Parker, a wanton and an unbeliever, is nonetheless irresistibly drawn to this unlipsticked puritan, who gives him little sexual encouragement either before or after marriage. Parker's enigmatic wooing and wedding of the woman he does not really love is an expression of his inner need to find what is missing in his life: a vital religious principle.

Likewise, the many tattoos with which he adorns his body over the years reflect his deep inner yearning to possess the secret which will make him other than he is. In the tattoo, he seeks the magic formula, the transforming design, which will endow him with mystical potency, magical attraction. In other words, Parker—though he resists the church—inwardly yearns for a spiritual transfiguring to match his outward alterations. The navy, the tattoos, the wife—all are reflections of the continuing search. All thus forewarn and prepare for the violent sanctification in the summer field.

Parker's conversion arises unexpectedly out of a farm "accident." The tractor overturns, the tree blazes forth, even Parker's own shoes (his former self) are consumed in flame. For Parker, the event is an undoubted miracle. As the tractor overturns, he yells " 'GOD ABOVE!' . . . if he had known how to cross himself he would have done it." From this point on, Parker is a radically changed man. He undergoes the typical convert's sense of the death of the old self. He is born anew, catapulted to a new identity and a destiny which seems directed by an outside hand. Hardly aware of what he is about, Parker seeks out the tattoo "artist" in town; there an inner voice directs him to the appropriate design—a stern Byzantine Christ—for his as yet undecorated back.

Parker's experience of unforeseen conversion, producing consequent revision of identity and purpose, follows the lines of many an unexpected awakening to the sense of God. The sacred illumination of Saint Francis, as interpreted by Evelyn Underhill, offers an interesting parallel. She first gives the account as it appears in Thomas of Celano's "Second Life" and then follows it with her own commentary:

> When this divided state, described by the legend as "the attempt to flee God's hand," had lasted for some years, it happened one day that he was walking in the country outside the gates of Assisi, and passed the little church of S. Damiano, "the which . . . was almost ruinous and forsaken of all men. And, being led by the Spirit, he went in to pray; and he fell down before the Crucifix in devout supplication, and *having been smitten by unwonted visitations, found himself another man than he who had gone in.*"
>
> Here, then, is the first stage of conversion. The struggle between two discrepant ideals of life has attained its term. A sudden and apparently "irrational" impulse to some decisive act reaches the surface-consciousness from the seething deeps. The impulse is followed; and the swift emergence of the transcendental sense results. This "unwonted visitation" effects an abrupt and involuntary alteration in the subject's consciousness: whereby he literally "finds himself another man." He is as one who has slept and now awakes. The crystallization of this new, at first fluid apprehension of Reality in the form of vision and audition: the pointing of the moral, the direct application of truth to the awakened self follow.[5]

After Parker's accident, he does not pause to analyze his experience: "He only knew that there had been a great change in his life, a leap forward into a worse unknown, and that there was nothing he could do about it. It was for all intents accomplished." At the tattoo artist's, he announces at once that he has come in search of a picture of God. He quickly thumbs past the inane representations of an affable Christ depicted as "The Good Shepherd, The Smiling Jesus, Jesus the Physician's Friend." He rejects all of these for "the haloed head of a flat stern Byzantine Christ with all-demanding eyes." Parker will have none of a soft Christianity which provides a vegetable love for all who wish to participate. He chooses rather the image of a stern and suffering God, whose promise is of a hard salvation through difficult paths. Above all, he is attracted to the eyes: "He felt as though, under their gaze, he was as transparent as the wing of a fly."

Parker, however, will not yet fully admit to himself or to the world the true nature of his experience. When the artist inquires whether he is saved and wishes to "testify" through his picture, Parker retorts that he has "no use for none of that." In the pool hall, Parker insists that he had the likeness put on merely "for laughs." A brawl erupts, and the men, sensing his dishonesty, throw him out "as if the barn-like room were the ship from which Jonah had been cast into the sea." At this stage, Parker, still denying the import of his experience, is indeed a Jonah, fleeing the god who has so unmistakably called him forth.

In an effort to win his wife's forgiveness for his indiscretion, Parker returns home and whispers his full name softly into the keyhole. The moment he accepts his true identity as a son of God, he is filled with transforming grace: " 'Obadiah,' he whispered and all at once he felt the light pouring through him, turning his spider web soul into a perfect arabesque of colors, a garden of trees and birds and beasts." In this final radiant moment, he is brought close to the center of a perfect creation.

Parker assumes that his wife will accept the image engraved on his back as final proof of his commitment to the Lord. Mrs. Parker, however, imbued as she is with fundamentalist doctrines of literal biblical interpretation, rejects him and his religious embellishment. ("It ain't anybody I know," she scoffs.) She throws him from the house, screaming accusations of idolatry after him; for she follows the Puritan view to its harsh extreme of rejecting any artistic production that smacks of idolatry. Parker, without knowing it, seeks, like the Byzantine artist, to capture the spirit and express it in visible form. Thrust outside, crying like a baby, he begins his participation in the sufferings of Christ, on whose Byzantine countenance welts have already begun to form.

Here, then, are three stories of revelation, each with a different manifestation and purpose. Asbury undergoes no violent visual or auditory revelation. His is predominantly the sense of presence, an awareness of the Holy Spirit descending to him as "purifying terror." Heaven opens in answer to Mrs. Turpin's question, and she perceives that the ranks of the blessed are not organized according to her personal standards of merit. Parker is captured by the Holy Spirit in a momentous revelation which leads him to conduct bizarre and incomprehensible even to himself. Yet, though the means differ, each experience is obviously a visitation of a sacred energy which chooses its own occasions to reveal itself and its own appropriate forms of discovery. In O'Connor's view, modern man is still susceptible to ancient forms of revelation. The authenticity of "miracle" is not a topic for debate but a fact evidenced repeatedly in human experience.

CHAPTER 8

Studies in Black and White

ALTHOUGH the "race question" as such does not play a prominant part in Flannery O'Connor's published fiction until relatively late in her career, the black man as a familiar feature of the Southern landscape and a commonplace element in Southern white experience is evident throughout her work.[1] Typical Southern attitudes are frequently revealed in casual comments or in passing allusions that betray entire systems of thought. The Grandmother of "A Good Man," for example, interrupts her running commentary on the "interesting" features of the landscape to note a black child standing by the highway:

> "Oh look at the cute little pickaninny!" she said and pointed to a Negro child standing in the door of a shack. "Wouldn't that make a picture, now?" she asked and they all turned and looked at the little Negro out of the back window. He waved.
> "He didn't have any britches on," June Star said.
> "He probably didn't have any," the grandmother explained. "Little niggers in the country don't have things like we do. If I could paint, I'd paint that picture," she said.

Two features of the Grandmother's reflections are significant: first, the black child is "cute"; second, his impoverished condition is not a subject for concern or sympathy, but merely a fact to be accepted as a feature of the social landscape, as much a part of this world as are the blue granite and red clay of the Georgia countryside. The characteristic white assumption of superiority is again reflected in Mrs. May's mistaken identification of the stray animal grazing in her yard as "some nigger's scrub bull" ("Greenleaf"). Mr. Fortune in "A View of the Woods," accusing his granddaughter of accumulating a secret miser's horde, taunts: "I bet you got it sewed up in your mattress . . . just like an old nigger woman."

In addition, the black character is defined through scenes in
which he himself enacts a minor but characteristic role. Most
often, his typical response is one of a sullen cooperation that
exasperates his white associate. In "A Circle in the Fire," one of
Mrs. Cope's continuing trials is the work habits of her black
helpers, who prefer to drive the tractor around the field rather
than take the bothersome precaution of raising the blade for
passing through the near gate. The black is especially contrary in
his dealings with the white who wants information from him.
None of the blacks in Tanner's gang ("Judgement Day") will
admit to acquaintance with the stranger idling near the sawmill:
"None of them knew who he was. They knew he didn't want to
work. They knew nothing else, not where he had come from, nor
why, though he was probably brother to one, cousin to all of
them." Old Mr. Fortune is forced to bribe the black boy at Tilman's with a nickel in order to find the whereabouts of his
granddaughter.

Thus, the white characters' attitudes toward the black are fixed
in terms of stereotype and cliché. The black, for his part, does
little to refute the stereotype. He obviously operates in accordance
with a *modus vivendi* long since adopted as a defense pattern
against a society which relegates him to an inferior status and
extends little hope for amelioration of his condition. He makes the
adjustments necessary for survival, and the white blithely accepts
his defensive stance as an attribute inborn in the race.

I Not Enough Real Ones: "The Artificial Nigger"

In two stories in the early collection, "The Artificial Nigger"
and "The Displaced Person," the black occupies a significant position, even though the major encounter is between whites rather
than between blacks and whites. In the first of these, "The Artificial Nigger," knowing the black is equated with worldly sophistication; and the journey to the city is, among other things, a
tentative initiation into acquaintance with the race.[2]

For the white boy Nelson, the journey is the archetypal voyage
into experience. Born in the city, but brought to the rural regions
while still an infant, he is determined to return to his birthplace
to discover for himself what is there. Mr. Head, his grandfather,
who is convinced that the city holds nothing of merit, intends

the trip to be an instruction in humility for Nelson so that he
will no longer boast of his superiority arising out of his cosmopolitan origin. It is, of course, Mr. Head who is instructed as a
result of the city experience. The story is basically a study in pride
(his), of its humbling, and of his ultimate forgiveness through the
operation of divine mercy.

Preparations for the journey begin at three-thirty in the morning when Mr. Head is awakened by the smell of the breakfast
being prepared by Nelson in the kitchen. This variation from
their customary routine is but one in a continuing series of
dislocations and disturbances, for going to the city means entering upon an unfamiliar experience in which one's previous identity
is temporarily dissolved in an unfamiliar milieu.

In the rural county where Nelson and his grandfather live,
blacks have been barred for many years. Thus, Nelson has reached
the threshold of adolescence without any firsthand experience
with blacks. His ignorance on this score leaves him open to his
grandfather's jeers and taunts, but Nelson expects that in the city
he will prove his ability to deal with the blacks and thus confirm his overall competence in the view of Mr. Head.

The first black man Nelson encounters appears on the train.
The black passenger is striking in his vulgarity, but it is doubtful
that Nelson is aware of this fact. Indeed, he proves totally incapable of interpreting his experience, for he fails to recognize
that the dark man is a black at all. Nelson excuses himself on the
grounds that the man is tan, rather than black. Nelson here is
introduced to the curious convention whereby various shades of
skin and gradations of blood are classed under the single category
of "Negro." After the grandfather smugly points out his mistake
to Nelson, the boy concludes that "the Negro had deliberately
walked down the aisle in order to make a fool of him and he
hated him with a fierce raw fresh hate. . . ."

In the city, despite all Mr. Head's careful efforts to keep the
station in view, the travelers ultimately find themselves lost in
a black section of town. Here, the two whites are like aliens
wandering without direction through a foreign country. Finally,
Nelson approaches a woman to ask directions; now, instead of
being repelled as he had been by the man on the train, he finds
himself pulled toward her by some strange magnetic force. Nelson, the motherless child, responds instinctively to the maternal

attractions of the black woman; but her attitude is mocking, superior; and after her explanations, the two whites are left as lost as before.

The betrayal scene, in which Mr. Head denies his grandson before the world, is shocking to both culprit and victim. Nelson, losing sight of his grandfather, runs in panic and knocks an elderly woman to the ground. When Mr. Head reappears, Nelson clings to him in terror, but Mr. Head announces to the startled crowd, "This is not my boy. . . . I never seen him before." Nelson is appalled by his grandfather's rejection, and Mr. Head is miserably aware of the magnitude of his failure: "He felt he knew now what time would be like without seasons and what heat would be like without light and what man would be like without salvation." This entire episode strongly suggests a dream sequence, a nightmare experience of a familiar world overturned. Their reconciliation occurs through a black man, not a real one but an imitation figure used as a lawn decoration. As they stare in mystified silence, Mr. Head delivers the pronouncement, "They ain't got enough real ones here. They got to have an artificial one." [3]

Mr. Head's observation, irrelevant as it seems, is sufficient to heal the breach separating the estranged pair.[4] His comment serves to "interpret" the meaning of the phenomenon and thus to restore the balance so rudely upset by his unjustifiable repudiation of Nelson earlier. Once again, he is the instructor and Nelson is the pupil. The child is obviously grateful to have his elder returned to the position of wisdom. The scorn of the statue that is implicit in Mr. Head's observation epitomizes the contempt which the two visitors feel toward the city itself, the large world which they can neither comprehend nor cope with. Through their rejection of the battered figure, they reassert their own superiority to all the dwellers of the "nigger heaven," and they claim once more their own identities which have been so badly assailed in the unfamiliar realm.

From the experience in the city, Nelson confirms for himself the basis of his grandfather's antipathy toward the great world. It is, however, Mr. Head himself who experiences the major instruction; for he discovers not only the depravity resident in his own soul but also the bounty of grace that permits forgiveness: "He had never thought himself a great sinner before but he saw now that his true depravity had been hidden from him lest it cause him despair. He realized that he was forgiven for sins from the beginning of time, when he had conceived in his own heart the sin of Adam, until the present, when he had denied poor Nelson. He saw that no sin was too monstrous for him to claim as his own, and since God loved in proportion as He forgave, he felt ready at that instant to enter Paradise." In essence, then, the story is one of instruction in mercy, without which man would be forever exiled to the realms of spiritual oblivion and perpetual despair.

II *In Collusion Forever: "The Displaced Person"*

The central theme of "The Displaced Person" is guilt and redemption, but the primary complication arises from the racial issue. The story develops as a sequence of betrayals, of which the whites' betrayal of the blacks reflects the larger betrayal of Christ by all humanity. Mr. Guizac's ignorance of American racial mores leads to a series of misunderstandings, which culminate in major disaster and universal guilt. In effect, the Pole dies because he fails to perceive that Christian *charitas* does not extend to marriage between white and black in the American South.

When the Displaced Person and his family arrive at the farm, Mrs. Shortley, the hired man's wife, stations herself on a nearby hill to observe the proceedings, and the black helpers watch from behind a mulberry tree. It is but natural that they should show an intense interest in what is happening, for they realize that the farm is a community where the fate of one involves the destinies of all. Mrs. McIntyre, the proprietress, sees herself as the mainstay of the operation: "I'm the one around here who holds all the strings together. . . . You're all dependent on me but you each and every one act like the shoe is on the other foot." Mrs. McIntyre, however, fails to perceive that her own welfare, both material and spiritual, is closely tied to that of her "dependents." The final action is one of mutual involvement in guilt and sorrow, and the consequences fall on each impartially.

The black helpers, Astor and Sulk, are a seemingly worthless pair, for they lie, steal, and exert themselves as little as possible; indeed they are barely articulate. Yet they fill their roles as workers at some minimal level. When Sulk fears they will be replaced

by the foreign workers, old Astor consoles him: "Never mind . . .
your place too low for anybody to dispute with you for it."

The white workers, though classed as superior according to
the Southern social structure, are, in fact, little better than the
blacks. Mr. Shortley, the hired man, will not take orders, smokes
in the barn, and operates a still on the sly. The blacks, too, have
a still on Mrs. McIntyre's land, and they and the Shortleys have
an unspoken understanding to respect the privacy of each other's
illegal operation.

Mr. Guizac, the Polish immigrant, is a vastly different type.
A model of proficiency, he can operate the various farm machines
with total dexterity, is an indefatigable worker, is scrupulously
clean, and does not even smoke. Mrs. McIntyre regards him as
her salvation, but he represents a definite threat to the Shortleys
and the blacks.

Within this group of mutually dependent persons there is a
marked lack of understanding. To Mrs. Shortley, Mr. Guizac
represents the unholy continent of Europe, which to her is "the
devil's experiment station." The notion of Europe calls to her mind
the nameless horrors of distant regions "where they had not advanced as in this country." She suspects that the Guizacs, like
rats carrying typhoid fleas, may bring contamination with them.
Mr. Guizac reminds Mr. Shortley of the man who had thrown a
grenade at him in the war, and he complains that it is unfair that
such persons should threaten the jobs of those like himself who
"fought and bled and died in the service of his native land."

Mr. Guizac too has difficulty comprehending unfamiliar aspects
of a strange society. He is impatient with the blacks, and he
makes the mistake of reporting to Mrs. McIntyre that he has
caught Sulk in the act of stealing a turkey from her pen. He is
troubled by Mrs. McIntyre's lack of concern and is confused by
her offhand explanation that "all Negroes would steal." But, despite Mr. Guizac's intolerance of certain black characteristics that
the native Southerners accept as inherent, he is only too accepting
in other ways. On his arrival, he shakes hands with the blacks as if
they were his equals. His democratic attitude violates Southern
notions of propriety and decency when he sets in motion a scheme
to bring his young niece to America as Sulk's bride. Mrs. McIntyre
has felt a growing irritation toward the Guizacs, even though they
have contributed substantially to her own material prosperity; but

her discovery that Guizac is plotting miscegenation causes her
to explode in indignation: "Mr. Guizac! You would bring this
poor innocent child over here and try to marry her to a half-
witted thieving black stinking nigger! What kind of a monster
are you!" She is unmoved by his protestations that the girl's
mother and father are dead, and that she has been confined in
an internment camp for three years. In the segregated South, marriage between white and black is impossible on any terms.

Thus, the misunderstandings arise not only from the provincial
whites' distorted notions of Europe and Europeans but also from
the foreigner's unwitting violations of the rigid Southern social
codes. In addition, there is a third level of misunderstanding, seen
in the vast discrepancy between ultimate spiritual reality and the
petty concerns of those obsessed with their own immediate material welfare. Father Flynn, the aging priest who automatically attempts to convert Mrs. McIntyre in the course of his visits, is a
reminder of the larger spiritual frame within which all human
action occurs. Father Flynn seems barely aware of the literal
features of experience, for his thoughts dwell constantly on salvation as expounded in the doctrines of the church. He alone responds to the deep symbolism of the peacocks strolling about the
farmyard; [5] to him, the magnificence of their spreading tails is
emblematic of the transfiguration. Mrs. McIntyre has no notion of
what he is talking about: "As far as I'm concerned . . . Christ was
just another D.P." Mrs. Shortley, viewing the peacocks earlier,
had also responded merely to the literal visual image.

Father Flynn's orthodox faith is contrasted with the bizarre
visions of Mrs. Shortley, who launches herself on a career of
apocalyptic revelation. In particular, she directs her sinister warnings against the Guizacs, who are, she insists, the devil's emis-
saries. Obviously, Mrs. Shortley's mantic trappings are an elaborate illusion bred out of her own sense of personal threat. Mrs.
Shortley ominously warns the blacks of their precarious position
before the invading "D.P.'s." She is surprised to discover that it
is her husband, rather than the black underlings, who is slated for
replacement. Without waiting for an official dismissal, she loads
their household goods, together with miscellaneous possessions
of Mrs. McIntyre, into their ancient car, and they leave before
the morning milking.

In the car, people and belongings are jumbled in a manner

curiously reminiscent of Mrs. Shortley's description of heaped European corpses. In the newsreel, she had seen "a small room piled high with bodies of dead naked people all in a heap, their arms and legs tangled together, a head trust in here, a head there, a foot, a knee, a part that should have been covered up sticking out, a hand raised clutching nothing." To Mrs. Shortley, the scene was vivid evidence of the devil's grip on Europe. When Mrs. Shortley was seized by the urge to prophesy, she had shouted: "Legs where arms should be, foot to face, ear in the palm of hand. Who will remain whole? Who?" As Mrs. Shortley succumbs to her stroke, she behaves in a strange manner: "She suddenly grabbed Mr. Shortley's elbow and Sarah Mae's foot at the same time and began to tug and pull on them as if she were trying to fit the two extra limbs onto herself." Mrs. Shortley does not "remain whole." She, too, proves vulnerable to disaster, like the unfortunate Europeans pictured in the distressing newsreel scene.

Mrs. Shortley becomes, therefore, in a very real sense a "displaced person": first, in her husband's loss of position, then in the wild frenzy of her death agony, and finally in her own loss of life. Further displacements arise through the demise of Mr. Guizac whose death occurs as a result of unpremeditated conspiracy on the part of the three observers, none of whom can bring himself to shout a warning to the man lying in the tractor's path: "She had felt her eyes and Mr. Shortley's eyes and the Negro's eyes come together in one look that froze them in collusion forever, and she had heard the little noise the Pole made as the tractor wheel broke his backbone."

As a result of their mutual participation in the "murder" of Mr. Guizac, the three culprits now become displaced persons themselves. Mr. Shortley leaves without notice that very night, and Sulk sets off unexpectedly for the southern part of the state. Mrs. McIntyre barely notices their absence, for she collapses and must be taken to the hospital. On her return home, she sells her cattle (at a loss) and lives her declining years enfeebled in mind and body. Her sole regular visitor is the priest, who comes faithfully once a week to feed the peacocks and to expound the mysteries of the Redeemer, Who remained so long a displaced person in the hearts of Mrs. McIntyre and her helpers.[6]

III   *A Failure in Communication*

In the second collection of stories, *Everything That Rises Must Converge*, the problem of racial maladjustments emerges as a specific concern in several stories. Now, new character types (both white and black) appear, reflecting the changed attitude of the races to the rapidly shifting racial conditions. In particular, two new situations are presented in these stories. The first deals with the sincere—but futile—efforts of the whites to communicate on more or less equal terms with their black associates in the new society (Mrs. Turpin in "Revelation" and Asbury in "The Enduring Chill"). In the second situation, the attempt proves not merely futile but fatal for the white instigator (Julian's mother in "Everything That Rises" and Tanner in "Judgement Day").

Mrs. Turpin, of "Revelation," after her trauma in the doctor's waiting room, seeks to share her deep hurt with the black laborers returning from the field; but their reassurances that she—being "sweet," "pretty," and "stout"—has been unfairly treated fail, as we have observed, to console her:

> Mrs. Turpin knew just exactly how much Negro flattery was worth and it added to her rage. "She said," she began again and finished this time with a fierce rush of breath, "that I was an old wart hog from hell."
> There was an astounded silence.
> "Where she at?" the youngest woman cried in a piercing voice. "Lemme see her. I'll kill her!"
> "I'll kill her with you!" the other one cried.
> "She b'long in the sylum," the old woman said emphatically. "You the sweetest white lady I know."
> "She pretty too," the other two said. "Stout as she can be and sweet. Jesus satisfied with her!"
> "Deed he is," the old woman declared.
> Idiots! Mrs. Turpin growled to herself. You could never say anything intelligent to a nigger. You could talk at them but not with them.

Asbury, of "The Enduring Chill," seizes on the notion of smoking with the black workers as his final significant action. The previous summer, he had induced the helpers to smoke with him in the barn and had attempted to persuade them to drink milk fresh from the cows, both in defiance of his mother's orders. The

helpers had refused, explaining merely that "She don't 'low it."
Asbury, however, had consumed the milk daily to show his
liberation from his mother's domination and his generous acceptance of the blacks as equals. From drinking the milk, he
contracts undulant fever.

The blacks miss the point of Asbury's determined sociability
in the dairy barn: "How come 'he talks so ugly about his ma?";
"She ain't whup him enough when he was little." Likewise, they
are confused as to the nature of their last visit with Asbury.
Convinced he has only hours remaining, Asbury has his mother
invite the employees in to say goodby: "He waited, preparing
himself for the encounter as a religious man might prepare himself for the last sacrament." When the blacks arrive, they stand
grinning in embarrassment, assuring Asbury over and over that
he "looks fine," despite his protestations that he is in fact dying.
His intended ritual of communal experience is thwarted, for the
helper to whom he offers the first cigarette assumes the entire
package is a gift and deposits it in his pocket. Asbury is thus
forced to produce another package for the second helper, who
plainly resents Asbury's apparent favoritism. The blacks leave,
continuing to assure Asbury of his healthy appearance; left alone,
"he knew that there would be no significant experience before
he died."

These two stories—"Revelation" and "The Enduring Chill"—
possess a common theme of spiritual illumination. The scenes with
the black characters are subordinate to the larger theme of enlightenment through grace, and the primary "convergences" are
thus spiritual rather than racial. The whites attempt—at times—
to break through the communication barrier to the black audience; but no real confrontation occurs because the participants
in the dialogue move along parallel tracks which permit no real
points of contact.

IV *The Price of Progress:*
"Everything That Rises Must Converge"

In two other stories in the second collection—"Everything That
Rises Must Converge" and "Judgement Day"—the emphasis centers on the black-white relation as such. They deal specifically
with the clash between the cultures in the form of physical vio-

lence released against a specific racial representative. In each case, the consequence is the annihilation of an older white person by a younger black. These—the opening and closing stories of the group—are crucial explorations of the potentially drastic consequences of the white-black encounter.

The title of the second collection—*Everything That Rises Must Converge*—is taken from Teilhard de Chardin, whose study of the biological processes of evolution convinced him that evolution itself is a continuing movement of various species into higher and higher forms of consciousness. Ultimately, these combine with or converge upon one another, in preparation for the final fusion of all being with supranatural consciousness at the "omega point." O'Connor gives the title an ironic twist: *convergence* in her title implies *collision;* and the stories deal, therefore, with such "convergences" in various areas: racial, social, and spiritual. The stories concerned with racial conflict reveal that, in the black's ascent of the social ladder, he eliminates certain of his white antagonists; for, as with Darwin, death is the price of failure to adapt to changing conditions of society.[7]

The title story revolves about the various racial attitudes of the central characters. The story is, in fact, simply the study of the interaction of these various states of mind; and the narrative ends with the elimination of one. The first point of view is that of Julian's mother, who is imbued with traditional Southern orthodoxy in all its various facets. She takes the black drive for integration as a personal affront, but she bears the black man no ill will as long as he "stays in his place" (in the back of the bus and on the other side of the fence). She is a woman with an amazing capacity to select the data of her personal "reality." A descendant of the Godhighs, an aristocratic slaveholding family, she maintains unperturbed her image of herself as a daughter of the aristocracy, even though she lives at present in a shabby neighborhood in a state of poverty barely genteel. Her illusions extend, of course, to her son Julian, whom she loyally introduces as a budding author who is getting his start by temporarily selling typewriters. Objecting to the changing social position of the blacks, she ignores the external evidence of that change; and that perversity costs her her life.

Julian, in contrast, prides himself on his enlightened views. He deliberately seats himself with black riders on the bus, and he desperately longs to strike up an "intellectual" conversation with his black acquaintances to demonstrate his unprejudiced and hence superior state of mind and spirit. He deliberately provokes his mother by flaunting her social standards, dallies with the thought of joining a "sit-in," and imagines with secret delight the pleasure of bringing a black woman home as his fiancée.

In truth, the son is a duplicate of his mother. Though outwardly he scoffs at her claims of aristocratic connections, inwardly he treasures the knowledge of his own superior heritage. To escape the pressures of the vulgar, uncomprehending society about him, he withdraws into an inner dream world, which is in fact an imaginary room of the lost family mansion. His ambitions to be an author obviously have little or no chance of realization. And it is unlikely that there is, as he claims, not a single person in a radius of three hundred miles worth knowing. His eagerly sought contacts with the blacks on the bus show the extent of his illusion. His "professional" black people turn out to be undertakers, and his chosen "equals" present him lottery tickets as they leave.

The mother is a representative of conservative Southern society, and the son—in his own view—of the younger progressives who seek to expiate the sins of the parents by openly accepting their "inferiors." The contest is played out ultimately in the drama of the final bus ride, where the opposing attitudes are tested with severe consequences for both mother and son. On the bus, the whites seek contact with the blacks (each in his own terms), which the latter pointedly reject. Julian, to emphasize his broad-mindedness and to annoy his mother, borrows matches from the black man next to him. It is an absurd gesture, since the bus carries a No Smoking sign and Julian does not smoke anyway. Julian's mother will not let the little black boy sitting beside her alone, and she tries to strike up a conversation with his mother, all the while making it obvious that she considers these people to be her inferiors. The black woman's resentment is pronounced. The mother, like Julian, is guilty of a gross intrusion of privacy, but neither perceives the fact that the overtures are unwelcome.

The hat plays a key symbolic function in the bus scene. The hat is striking on two counts: (1) it is a monstrosity (purple flaps flanking an empty green cushion) and (2) it is, in the mother's economy, an expensive purchase (she could have paid the gas bill with the $7.50 the hat cost). The fact that the black woman has also selected the hat reveals that the blacks' economic status is rapidly overtaking that of the whites' and that the blacks have won as much freedom to pursue absurdity as the whites. The hat clearly signifies the "doubling" of the white and black women. The exchange of roles is further suggested by the seating arrangements, whereby the women seem to "exchange sons." The white woman clearly resents her son's being positioned next to the black mother, but the latter is obviously even more vexed by her own offspring's proximity to the white matron. Julian, of course, enjoys the situation immensely, and he hopes that the entire experience—especially the twin hat—will prove a good lesson to his mother.

The action which provokes the final assault upon Julian's mother is her thoughtless presentation of money to the little black boy after they all leave the bus. When she successfully bestows her penny upon the child, she is totally oblivious of the insult she delivers with the coin: the gesture is "as natural to her as breathing." The black woman is not disposed to accept the insult of charity. Her response is immediate, violent, instinctive: "Then all at once she seemed to explode like a piece of machinery that had been given one ounce of pressure too much." She aims a powerful blow with her fist and sends the mother to the sidewalk.

At this point, the black mother and her child disappear down the street and out of the story. Julian, who is initially pleased that his mother has finally gotten the lesson she deserves, presents a detailed interpretation of the meaning of that lesson:

"Don't think that was just an uppity Negro woman," he said. "That was the whole colored race which will no longer take your condescending pennies. That was your black double. . . . What all this means," he said, "is that the old world is gone. The old manners are obsolete and your graciousness is not worth a damn."

.   .   .

"You needn't act as if the world had come to an end," he said, "because it hasn't. From now on you've got to live in a new world and face a few realities for a change. Buck up," he said, "it won't kill you."

But, of course, it already has.

Julian thus learns that human imperfections are extended to all in the democracy of the races; that the deficiencies of age and social short-sightedness can beget consequences totally out of proportion to their intentions; and that, in order to embrace his new friends, he may be required to sacrifice his own family. A lesson is, indeed, implicit in thé black woman's violent action; but the pupil is Julian who is brought at last to instruction in guilt and sorrow.

Flannery O'Connor obviously is not in this story presenting solutions to social problems, nor is she endorsing particular positions or attitudes. She is impartial in her stern evaluation and judgment; to her, the biased Southerner clinging to outmoded perception, the enthusiastic liberal eager to demonstrate his goodwill, and the sullen black resentful of white overtures are all examples of pride, absurdity, and vice. The work is a warning and an admonition to all involved—there is no major culprit to be singled out and set against the others. The villain is lack of compassion, failure of sympathy, and, as such, it resides in the souls of all, black and white, young and old.

V   *Ship Express Collect: "Judgement Day"*

"Judgement Day," the closing story of *Everything That Rises Must Converge*, likewise focuses on the question of racial adjustments. As in the title story, a representative of the older generation, unable to adapt to the changed social patterns of a transformed world, provokes the wrath of an "emancipated" black and pays for his social obtuseness with his life.

"Judgement Day" is unique among O'Connor's collected works because it alone is set in the North. This shift in setting is significant, because now we view for the first time the conflict between Southern rural and Northern cosmopolitan; in this conflict are summed up many of the social problems that beset our age.

The first of these is the problem encountered in the move from country to city. In the South, Tanner, a white man, lived in a shack. It was, furthermore, a squatter's shack, built on another man's property and shared with a black, a "stinking skin full of bones." But at least the shack had air around it, and at least one could put his feet on the ground. His poverty has forced Tanner to move to New York City to live with his daughter. In the city, people live in pigeon-hutches, and the air is fit only "for cats and garbage." Tanner himself quickly rejects the advantages of the city: "He never wanted to set foot again on the underground railroad or the steps that moved under you while you stood still or any elevator to the thirty-fourth floor."

More important in the story, however, is the examination of the races themselves and their mutual relationship. There are three major black characters, each representative of a type or class. The first of these—Coleman—reflects, like the lumber gang bossed by Tanner, the typical stereotype of the Southern Negro—slightly ludicrous, slightly pathetic, easily dominated by the determined white with his "superior brain power." His initial hostility eased by Tanner's gift of the mock-glasses, Coleman becomes Tanner's friend for life. When Tanner's daughter shames her father for living with a black man, he hotly defends the arrangement. "Who you think cooks? Who you think cuts my firewood and empties my slops? He's paroled to me. That no good scoundrel has been on my hands for thirty years. He ain't a bad nigger." The last, of course, is a gross understatement of Tanner's private views. Coleman is Tanner's one and only close friend, the single person he writes from New York, the one he speaks to in his imagination when he recounts his unwholesome experiences in the city, and the one he addresses his corpse to in case he should die on his way home: "IF FOUND DEAD SHIP EXPRESS COLLECT TO COLEMAN PARRUM, CORINTH, GEORGIA."

Coleman is, in fact, Tanner's twin.[8] When he first laid eyes on Coleman, Tanner "had an instant's sensation of seeing before him a negative image of himself, as if clownishness and captivity had been their common lot." The similarity of the two men is further reinforced by their physiological development: "When Coleman was young, he looked like a bear; now that he was old he looked like a monkey. With Tanner it was the opposite; when he was young he had looked like a monkey but when he got old, he looked like a bear."

The two men live together in their shack on terms of closest friendship. The friendship is made possible by the fact that each accepts a mutually agreed upon structure of ground rules: Tanner, as the white, is supposedly the superior. The difference in color between them will never be ignored, though obviously it has long since ceased to matter. Tanner's ability to "handle niggers" proceeds from a certain set of assumptions as to their inherent character and the appropriate means of dealing with them. As long as they fall into the role chosen for them and submit to the prescribed forms of treatment, all goes well and harmony prevails between the races.

Tanner's first major difficulty in dealing with a Southern black comes with "Dr." Foley, who owns the land on which Tanner and Coleman live. Dr. Foley is obviously of a new breed. He is an opportunist who competes with great success in the white middle-class race for "things." Most of his profit is derived from his own race, which he exploits as fully as might a white man: "He was everything to the niggers—druggist and undertaker and general counsel and real estate man and sometimes he got the evil eye off them and sometimes he put it on." Dr. Foley, in fact, is only part black, the rest being Indian and white. But, to Tanner, his black blood determines his race. And Tanner is determined not to stay on Foley's land on Foley's terms. Looking back, he realizes that he should have opted for being a "nigger's white nigger" rather than take his daughter's offer of living in the noplace of New York City.

The third black type is that depicted in the characters of the black actor and his wife, who move into the apartment next to the daughter's. They are unlike anything ever experienced by Tanner, and his failure to recognize this fact leads to his death. Tanner's great pride is that he has always been successful in "handling niggers." He is now too old to learn new ways of thought and behavior; he is like an animal who relies on some previously learned response pattern in a new and inappropriate situation, with fatal results.

In order for it to be seen in its full significance, the behavior of the black actor toward Tanner must be set against other patterns of human relationship within the story. There is, first, the relationship of Tanner and Coleman, who, though of different races, obviously lived together in mutual affection and respect. The daughter, contemptuous of Tanner's lowering himself by settling in "with niggers," takes him North as a matter of pride. Dr. Foley warns him of the treatment he can expect: " 'She don't want no old daddy like you,' he said. 'Maybe she say she do, but that ain't likely. Even if you rich,' he said, 'they don't want you.

They got they own ideas. . . .'" Dr. Foley, of course, is right; Tanner finds his daughter's attitude of righteous solicitude unbearable.

Just as Tanner's open acceptance of responsibility for Coleman is contrasted with his daughter's resentful attitude toward him, his essentially peaceful method of dealing with the black labor gang he had supervised is contrasted with the actor's violent reaction to him. The actor first ignores him, then splutters denials of Tanner's assertions that he (the actor) comes from South Alabama, and finally erupts in outraged violence against his "accuser." Admittedly, the black man has much provocation for his action. Yet, in this situation, he is manifestly the intellectual superior, and he evidences none of the compassion nor kindness that Tanner had displayed in like situations when his was the superior mind. Further, it is ironic that the very methods that probably saved Tanner's life in his initial dealings with Coleman lose it for him here. The black man's answer to Tanner's overtures is to slam the old man into the wall, bringing on the stroke from which he never recovers. Later, discovering the old man helpless on the staircase, the actor stuffs his head and limbs through the bannisters and leaves him there to die. The black man, in fact, no longer behaves like a human being. He acts from a single impulse, uncontrolled fury against the whites, and the old man becomes his inadvertent target.

Significant also are Tanner's religious attitudes contrasted with those of his daughter and of the black neighbor. Both the latter are "emancipated" from provincial religious commitments. The daughter disdains traditional belief: "And don't throw hell at me. I don't believe in it. That's a lot of hardshell Baptist hooey." When Tanner addresses the actor as "preacher," the latter protests, "And I'm not no preacher! I'm not even no Christian. I don't believe that crap. There ain't no Jesus and there ain't no God." Thus, the "new" blacks and Tanner's daughter have much in common. Their renunciation of religious belief obviously underlies their lack of humanity. And each, in effect, murders the old man: she, spiritually; he, physically.

The title obviously has various significances within the work. Tanner dreams of having himself shipped back to Georgia in a pine coffin. Once there, he will spring out of the coffin to surprise Coleman and Hooten with gleeful shouts of "Judgement Day!

Judgement Day!" In the delirium of his last moments, Tanner
imagines he is playing such a role. When he finally recognizes
the strange neighbor, he makes the fatal mistake of repeating
the hated title of preacher. This apparently so incenses the actor
that he decides it is, indeed, Judgment Day for the detested old
man. The death of Tanner, however, makes it a day of judgment
for the survivors as well as the deceased, for everyone in the narrative is being subjected to close scrutiny and evaluation by author and audience. Tanner himself suggests the terms: "The
Judgement is coming."

Interestingly, this last story of Flannery O'Connor is actually
a recasting of her first published narration, "The Geranium,"
which was written during her student days at Iowa and published in *Accent* (Summer, 1946); but major changes occur from
first to final form. In the early effort, O'Connor uncharacteristi-
cally employs a highly contrived symbol—the geranium itself,
whose uprootedness corresponds to that of the old man unsuc-
cessfully transplanted to the Northern metropolis. The previous
association of "Dudley" (Tanner) with the Southern blacks of
his home was less intimate—his friend lived in the same residence
with him but in the status of servant assigned to basement quarters. And, most significant, the black Northern neighbor is depicted as a genteel, modestly dressed liberal, whose offense is a
gratuitous act of kindness to the aging Southerner—he generously
assists Dudley up the apartment stairs. Dudley does not die from
his experience, but he is severely shaken by the disturbing reversal of the usual white-black relationship. The emphasis in the
first version is thus on the new role of equality which casts the
black as potential savior rather than as villain.

"Everything That Rises" and "Judgement Day" do not deal
with the "race issue" as a sociological problem but with the difficulty of adjustment on the level of personal encounter. When
asked specifically about the relation of the races in the South,
O'Connor observed that

> It requires considerable grace for two races to live together,
> particularly when the population is divided about fifty-fifty be-
> tween them and when they have our particular history. It can't
> be done without a code of manners based on mutual charity.
> I remember a sentence from an essay of Marshall McLuhan's.
> I forget the exact words but the gist of it was, as I recollect it,
> that after the Civil War, formality became a condition of survival.

This doesn't seem to me any less true today. Formality preserves that individual privacy which everybody needs and, in these times, is always in danger of losing. It's particularly necessary to have in order to protect the rights of both races. When you have a code of manners based on charity, then when the charity fails—as it is going to do constantly—you've got those manners there to preserve each race from small intrusions upon the other. The uneducated Southern Negro is not the clown he's made out to be. He's a man of very elaborate manners and great formality which he uses superbly for his own protection and to insure his own privacy. All this may not be ideal, but the Southerner has enough sense not to ask for the ideal but only for the possible, the workable. The South has survived in the past because its manners, however lopsided or inadequate they may have been, provided enough social discipline to hold us together and give us an indentity. Now those old manners are obsolete, but the new manners will have to be based on what was best in the old ones —in their real basis of charity and necessity. In practice, the Southerner seldom underestimates his own capacity for evil. For the rest of the country, the race problem is settled when the Negro has his rights, but for the Southerner, whether he's white or colored, that's only the beginning. The South has to evolve a way of life in which the two races can live together with mutual forebearance. You don't form a committee to do this or pass a resolution; both races have to work it out the hard way. In parts of the South these new manners are evolving in a very satisfactory way, but good manners seldom make the papers.[9]

Whatever her personal feelings toward the blacks may have been, Flannery O'Connor seemed determined not to let any soft liberal "sentimentalism" weaken her fiction. Her attitudes toward the blacks are set in the same harsh lines of judgment that she displays toward the whites. Universal guilt by definition extends to all races and permeates all blood lines. If the black woman on the bus errs in her violence against the mother, then Julian too is at fault for his failure to empathize with the plight of those who are too old to change. If the city actor is abominable in his violent response to the old man's overtures, the daughter is likewise contemptible in her casual disregard of her filial commitment. The old are pathetic, and, in terms of the new society, expendable. Their ways are outmoded, their attitudes indefensible, but it is they who will bear the brunt of suffering when they collide with the forces shaping the new world.

CHAPTER 9

Variations on a Theme

THE stories in *Everything That Rises Must Converge* so far discussed deal with various religious and racial "convergences" leading to either annihilation or salvation. A final group remains to be considered: three stories depicting the clashes occasioned by mounting economic and social pressures within a shifting Southern society. All are concerned, in one way or another, with the motif of property: property threatened ("Greenleaf"), property sold ("A View of the Woods"), and property (privacy) invaded ("The Comforts of Home"). [1]

In one sense, all these stories are retellings or variations of earlier writings, with repetition of familiar themes, characters, and motifs. [2] "Greenleaf" is a kind of inverted "Displaced Person," with the farm widow, rather than her employee, now the victim. "A View of the Woods," like "The Artificial Nigger," depicts the split between the generations, but the element of healing grace is absent. Thomas, of "The Comforts of Home," is a kind of male Hulga; the story suggests what might have happened had the Bible salesman taken up residence within her house. The characters themselves are drawn mostly from the by-now familiar types: the widow struggling to wrest a living from her second-rate farm; the superstitious tenant wife, indulging in visions and orgies; the stubborn old man, convinced of his own infallibility; the ineffectual son unable to declare his independence from the self-sacrificing mother.

I *"Greenleaf": Property Threatened*

Mrs. May, of "Greenleaf," shares many obvious affinities with other O'Connor characters. She herself is—like Mrs. Cope, Mrs. Hopewell, and Mrs. McIntyre—a widow trying desperately to manage a rather makeshift farm in order to provide for herself and her dependents. Like the other widows, she is plagued by irresponsible help whom she must cannily supervise in order to hold the operation together. She too feels that the world at large is in conspiracy against her. Her employees, the forces of nature, her family—all are threats to her well-being; only through her own shrewd perspicacity is she able to outwit the destructive elements which surround her and to eke out her survival.

Mrs. May, like her counterparts, suffers from a series of obvious character defects. Her determined efforts to survive lead her to an obsessive concern with the world of things—her personal possessions, the land, the stock, and the tools essential to the operation of the farm. Although she is outwardly a religious conformist, inwardly she rejects all binding spiritual commitment: "She was a good Christian woman with a large respect for religion, though she did not, of course, believe any of it was true." The consequence of her narrow concern for her own immediate welfare is a lack of compassion for those about her. She views her hired man as an instrument, a *thing* like the farm machines, whose sole function is to contribute to her own welfare. She bears with his insolence and continuing inefficiency (the fields sometimes come up in clover instead of rye when Mr. Greenleaf puts the wrong seeds in the machine) because she feels she has no real choice.

Along with her excessive devotion to her "property," Mrs. May suffers from an acute sense of her own superiority; she scorns the Greenleaf family as obvious white trash. The entire family communicates in a species of sub-English peculiar to themselves; their children are dirty; and Mrs. Greenleaf senior dips snuff and engages in orgiastic ceremonies of "prayer healing":

> Every day she cut all the morbid stories out of the newspaper —the accounts of women who had been raped and criminals who had escaped and children who had been burned and of train wrecks and plane crashes and the divorces of movie stars. She took these to the woods and dug a hole and buried them and then she fell on the ground over them and mumbled and groaned for an hour or so, moving her huge arms back and forth under her and out again and finally just lying down flat and, Mrs. May suspected, going to sleep in the dirt.

When the stray Greenleaf bull invades her grounds, Mrs. May is especially offended because she feels it shows a marked ingratitude on their parts for the many generosities she has extended to them in the past: " 'If I recall, they wore my boys' old clothes and played with my boys' old toys and hunted with my boys' old guns. They swam in my pond and shot my birds and fished in my stream and I never forgot their birthday and Christmas seemed to roll around very often if I remember it right. And do they think of any of those things now?' she asked. 'NOOOOO,' she said."

In particular, Mrs. May is convinced of the superiority of her own two sons, Wesley and Scofield, to the Greenleaf twins. In her view, her boys are highly successful, even though one teaches in a second-class university, grumbling each day about the twenty-mile drive to and from a job he hates, and the other makes his living selling "nigger-policy" insurance. Although they are in their thirties, neither son shows any inclination to accept the responsibilities of a wife and independent household, nor do they contribute to the management of their mother's farm.

The Greenleaf boys, by contrast, are obviously on their way up. They have taken advantage of the benefits available to them from their war service, studying agriculture at the university and building a brick duplex which, although it looks like a warehouse with windows, is still the kind of house everyone else is building. They have also broken through the provincial attitudes which characterize Mrs. May and her sons by marrying French wives. Mrs. May's great illumination as to the extent of the Greenleafs' achievement as dairy farmers comes when she surreptitiously inspects their milking parlor: "She opened the milking room door and stuck her head in and for the first second she felt as if she were going to lose her breath. The spotless white concrete room was filled with sunlight that came from a row of windows head-high along both walls. The metal stanchions gleamed ferociously and she had to squint to be able to look at all."

Thus, in the two families we have near-allegorical types of the Old and New South. Mrs. May's pride develops out of her sense of superiority as a property owner, one who heads an established family with a secure position in the local social hierarchy. But the South is in a highly fluid state. The Greenleafs are the Snopeses of the postwar world; and, like Faulkner's tribe, they are un-

stoppable in their rise to power. The Greenleafs are in the as-
cendent because they possess the vitality and imagination which
have disappeared from the "respectable" classes. In a dismal pre-
monition, Mrs. May foresees the future consequences: in twenty
years, the Greenleafs will have become "society."

The death of Mrs. May is immediately prepared for by a dual
foreshadowing. On the way to the pasture, Mrs. May detects in
Mr. Greenleaf's evident hostility a veiled wish to shoot her instead of the stray bull. Later, while waiting at the car for Mr.
Greenleaf to re-emerge from the woods, she toys with the thought
that the animal has gored his pursuer against a tree: "She thought
of it almost with pleasure as if she had hit on the perfect ending
for a story she was telling her friends." It is, of course, Mrs. May
who provides the "perfect ending"—at least as the story might
have been told from the Greenleaf point of view, for she herself
is gored to death by the bull. On the literal level, Mrs. May's
death, like that of Mr. Guizac earlier, can be attributed to many
but assigned to no one in particular. The guilt extends to her in-
dolent sons, who refuse to share the responsibility for the bull
just as they refuse to help with any of the work on the farm; to
the indifferent Greenleaf twins, who leave the harried widow to
cope with the consequences of their neglect; and to the uncoop-
erative hired man, who arrives too late to save the hapless victim.

Interestingly, the death itself is presented in the imagery of
lover and beloved. When Mrs. May had first noted the bull in her
yard, he had stood in the moonlight "like some patient god come
down to woo her." When he discovers her in the midst of the
field, he gallops toward her "with a gay almost rocking gait as if
he were overjoyed to find her again." And, when the bull attacks
her, he buries "his head in her lap, like a wild tormented lover."
In this equation of death and love, Flannery O'Connor is turning
to a familiar imaginative archetype. Renaissance writers often
cast the abstract concept of death in the role of the insistent
suitor. Freud emphasized the affinities of Eros with Thanatos, the
warring life-death impulses that constantly struggle for ascen-
dency. The significance of the twin motif in American literature
has been noted by Leslie Fiedler in his *Love and Death in the
American Novel,* and its implications for Western history have
been explored by Norman O. Brown in *Life Against Death.* Although the close affinity of love and death has long been appar-

ent, as evidenced both in literature and in universal human experience, the equation of the two in the work of Flannery O'Connor is unusual. In this particular story, she chooses to view death in a traditional aspect which is but one among many perspectives presented in her various employments of the theme.

The Greenleaf bull is, of course, more than a poetic embodiment of the dualistic love-death concept. He becomes, in one sense, the executor of a "divine" sentence. Mrs. May, like others in the long catalogue of O'Connor "victims," is struck down as if in retribution for her lifelong dedication to blinding pride. More immediately, he becomes, by links of ownership, the instrument of Greenleaf vengeance against a hardhearted exploiter. The bull is Greenleaf property, and his abrupt annihilation of Mrs. May prefigures the Greenleaf takeover of a world traditionally dominated by "Mays." The demise of Mrs. May strongly suggests, therefore, the radical social transformation currently at work in the South.

Mrs. May discovers at last that her cherished property is no protection against calamity. Her face in death is full of discovery, of awareness of her own vulnerability, and of the triumph of the Greenleafs. As the bull sinks his horns into the heart so long inured to the demands of human charity, she assumes "the look of a person whose sight has been suddenly restored but who finds the light unbearable."

II "A View of the Woods": Property Sold

In "A View of the Woods," property becomes a weapon employed in the war of ego. Old man Fortune permits his daughter and her husband Pitts to live on his farm, but he never lets them forget who owns it. He will not allow them to dig a well, nor will he accept rent from them because he so thoroughly relishes the notion that they are fully dependent upon him. Mr. Fortune delights to sell off his land in pieces, all in the name of "progress": "He wanted to see a paved highway in front of his house with plenty of new-model cars on it, he wanted to see a supermarket store across the road from him, he wanted to see a gas station, a motel, a drive-in picture-show within easy distance." Mr. Fortune prides himself that he is "a man of advanced vision, even if he was seventy-nine years old."

In particular, Mr. Fortune enjoys baiting his hapless son-in-law, who watches helplessly as the farm dwindles through the old man's successive transactions. In Mr. Fortune's eyes his son-in-law, not being Mr. Fortune, is an idiot, the sort who "would let a cow pasture or a mule lot or a row of beans interfere with progress." In his constant goading of Pitts, Mr. Fortune revels in the keen pleasures of self-assertion and pride. C. S. Lewis gives an account of the more serious orders of sin which is an effective commentary on the behavior indulged in by this tyrant-miser: "All the worst pleasures are purely spiritual: the pleasure of putting other people in the wrong, of bossing and patronizing and spoiling sport, and backbiting; the pleasures of power, of hatred." [3]

The crisis of the story arises when Fortune proposes to sell the "front lawn" for a filling station. Again, he argues that this will serve the cause of progress, and he points out the convenience of having gas and groceries available just outside the front door. The purchaser is Tilman, and we get some notion of what may be expected to appear on the property from the description of Tilman's present enterprise, with its jumble of wrecked autos, stone chickens, tombstones, and dance hall, all adjacent to his country store and filling station. Tilman's operation epitomizes nature assaulted and transformed by modern commercialism.

Fortune, who hates his son-in-law because the latter took from him a piece of property (Fortune's daughter), adores the youngest Pitts child and considers her his special possession; she is a tiny duplicate of her grandfather in both looks and action. Fortune strives to dominate his granddaughter in every way, determined to breed all traces of Pitts out of her so that she will emerge "pure Fortune." He is incensed by the father's efforts to discipline her and irked by her apparent willingness to submit to her parent's authority. The grandfather sees in her submission a betrayal of her identity as a Fortune, and he finally decides to assume himself the full authoritarian role.

Mary Fortune Pitts, whose name indicates her divided role, vacillates in her loyalties between parent and grandparent. She attempts to block the old man's plans for selling the front property by pointing out that the loss of the plot will cut off the family's "view of the woods." Her secret loyalties to her father are revealed in her final protest that this area is where he grazes his calves. Pitts, on the other hand, is convinced that Mary Fortune is behind the entire scheme to sell, and he deals her a sound beating for her supposed connivings. When she discovers that her grandfather has actually consummated the appalling transaction, she hurls bottles at the frightened purchaser to vent her anger.

Finally, Mr. Fortune decides that he will have to use physical force to quell his granddaughter's spirit. In return, she attacks him violently, knocking him to the ground. The ultimate consequence of the encounter is the death of both participants, the final destruction of both Fortune and his "property." Because the two so closely resemble each other, the fight strongly suggests an act of mutual suicide. When Mary Fortune bites his jaw, Mr. Fortune seems "to see his own face coming to bite him from several sides at once." Lying prone in the dust, Mr. Fortune stares at his own image glaring down at him, "pale identical eye" looking into "pale identical eye." But the image, "triumphant and hostile," declares "You been whipped . . . by me . . . and I'm PURE Pitts." The old man cannot, of course, tolerate this insult. In his fury, he slams his granddaughter's skull against a rock, killing her; he himself expires shortly thereafter from a heart attack. In the end, both Fortune and Pitts are annihilated; nothing is left but the yellow monster-machine nearby, "gorging itself on clay."

The religious dimension of the work, though not heavily emphasized, is introduced in Mr. Fortune's earlier vision of the woods at sunset, seeming to rise from pools of red "as if someone were wounded behind the woods and the trees were bathed in blood." Again we are reminded of humanity's perpetual assault upon Christ and of His continuing sorrow for its indifferent rejection of His message. For Mr. Fortune, love implies not a turning away from, but a movement into, self. When that inward center is reached, he places himself in total isolation from the Holy Spirit; and the consequence is death, spiritual and physical. For him, the mystery reflected in the reddening woods suggests not a vision of heaven but a view of hell.

III   *"The Comforts of Home": Property (Privacy) Invaded*

"The Comforts of Home" is a story also concerned with "property," but in the sense of a personal privacy invaded by an upsetting outside agent. Once more, we encounter the pairing of the exasperating widow and her dependent intellectual son, the latter now cast as a historian of local events. The depiction of an orderly household unsettled by the outside intruder recalls similar situations in "The Lame Shall Enter First" and in "A Circle in the Fire." Again, there is emphasis on the meaning of "place" (home, position), and the story ends with the displacement of the two "householders," one now dead and the other a matricide.

Four of the stories in the second collection examine the mother-son pattern; three of these end with the death of the mother. In each instance, the son is partly to blame, either metaphorically or literally. In stories such as "Everything That Rises Must Converge" and "Greenleaf," O'Connor strongly implies that the callous unconcern of children for their parents can have disastrous consequences. In "The Comforts of Home," the son himself (Thomas) pulls the trigger; thus, he literally becomes the direct agent of his own mother's death.

One view of satire holds that all practitioners of the art are in effect seeking to "kill the mother" through their works.[4] The antagonisms first aroused in the nursery by the "mother tyrant" are later unleashed against an objectionable society whose imperfections are no longer tolerable. The mother is, of course, the first representative of the "not-self," the society which surrounds and sustains us, but which at the same time restricts and limits us in our activities. The mother, like the world outside, provides the actual supports for our existence. We recognize our debt of gratitude, but at the same time we charge her with her obvious shortcomings, for which we feel she must be punished. In essence, she sums up the spiritual and social milieu which is our heritage.

Flannery O'Connor strikes at almost every aspect of her society—its vanities, foibles, and ignorant pacts with evil. Her stern castigations suggest both her scorn and love for her region, for the unique matrix of time and place which helped shape her own identity. Her various depictions of matricide are, I think, closely bound to her ambivalent attitudes toward the South itself—outrage at its follies, guilt at the seeming inner disloyalty revealed thereby.

The attack upon the mother reflects one's dissatisfaction with exterior society, but at the same time it suggests as well an assault upon the self. Our own identity is inextricably involved with that of the parent. When we turn upon her, we are much

like Mr. Fortune, who in destroying his granddaughter, kills himself as his twin. If we survive the conflict, we are left with the
remorseful recognition that we have killed what we most loved.
In psychological terms, these various depictions of matricide
are like deeply buried hostilities finding expression in dream fantasy; the release of aggression is followed by a predictable sense
of remorse and guilt. Again and again, the child turns upon the
parent or through spiritual withdrawal permits the parent to be
exposed to ruinous assailants. The parent figure—though she nags,
whines, and infuriates—almost never turns against the child. The
one exception is Mr. Fortune, who attacks his beloved granddaughter, but only because he is so passionately intent on destroying his enemy "Pitts" that he forgets that the child is also
"Fortune."

Certain ambiguities arise in connection with all of these stories,
especially "The Comforts of Home." Typically, we can discover
some character whose inclinations are preferable, or some course
of behavior, real or implied, which can avert disaster. In "The
Comforts of Home" all ways seem equally deficient, all choices
similarly objectionable. Thomas, the ultimate culprit, is caught
between the two extremes of action and inaction. Neither course
is a solution to his problem. Failure to act is to continue in his
old, ineffective ways, offering further proof of his unmanliness.
Sarah Ham (alias Star Drake) threatens home and identity. Unless he can rouse himself, she will ursurp his place, and he will
have to find new quarters, an unbearable prospect.

The consequences of following his deceased father's counsels
to aggressive action are likewise unsatisfactory, but Thomas al-
lows himself to be guided by this inner voice down to the fatal
command "Fire!" If, indeed, Thomas is being led by his father's
spirit, it is a ghost deeply corrupted, since the course of his advice leads straight to calamity. When, like Hamlet, Thomas finally
acts, it is to destroy both an unintended victim and himself. More
likely, Thomas is deluded, for this ghost, strongly reminiscent of
the stranger who taunts Tarwater, suggests either the devil himself in the guise of the parent, or, more likely, an overcompensa-
tion on Thomas's part for his failure to assume a properly mascu-
line role in the house after his father's death.

The mother suffers from an "excess of virtue," an exaggerated
charity which fails to recognize that whoever dabbles in "evil" is

likely to suffer its contaminations. The mother is an innocent intent on salvaging at least some of the world, but she is unaware of the potential dangers inherent in her action. She, like the social workers and psychiatric counselors O'Connor so frequently indicts, wishes to regenerate society through an abundance of good-will.[5] However, before we condemn her too strongly, we should recall the numerous characters elsewhere in the narratives who are charged with the opposite flaw—a callous insensitivity to the needs of others.

The girl herself poses perhaps the most difficult problem in understanding. Her rampant sexuality suggests, considering O'Connor's typical attitudes, a representation of pure evil, but the accusation is difficult to sustain because she is said to be lacking in the "moral faculty." The lawyer consulted by Thomas's mother explains that "the girl was a psychopathic personality not insane enough for the asylum, not criminal enough for the jail, not stable enough for society." Thomas knows that she embodies "the very stuff of corruption, but blameless corruption because there was no responsible faculty behind it. He was looking at the most unendurable form of innocence. Absently he asked himself what the attitude of God was to this, meaning if possible to adopt it."

Flannery O'Connor's characters insist again and again that there is no mid-region between Christ and the devil, no neutral zone between good and evil. If we now accept Thomas's assessment of this social misfit, we are confronted by a moral universe suddenly grown vastly more complex. This apparent leniency or compromise with modernist positions would seem to deny the absolutism of O'Connor's moral vision elsewhere.

If the author impartially indicts all the characters and rejects all paths of action, the story appears to lack a moral center. Certainly, such moral neutrality is a common feature of modern literature, but it is highly untypical of Flannery O'Connor's work. We have suggested earlier that a counterthrust constantly works to challenge the spiritual affirmation of her narratives. Perhaps here we have evidence of the strong inroads made by her opposing vision. The author seems to swing toward a position of relativity which she herself so steadfastly denied. What is left is irony stripped of its anagogical implications. We confront a vision still stern, but one distanced considerable from its spiritual base,

Thomas's inadvertent killing of his mother thus becomes merely a bizarre melodrama, not an event carrying deep tragic or spiritual implications. We are tempted to agree with Thomas, who "damned not only the girl but the entire order of the universe that made her possible."

However, such a seemingly abrupt reversal of moral perspective on the author's part is probably deceptive. More likely, her rejection of the various characters and their misguided actions stems from their own separation from Christian concerns. The mother's efforts to help the girl are misdirected precisely because no religious commitment controls her actions. Like Sheppard in "The Lame Shall Enter First," she is "good" but she is not "right." She, like Sarah Ham and Thomas and most of the other residents in the earthly city, is afflicted with the "blindness of those who don't know they cannot see."

As I noted earlier, many stories in *Everything That Rises Must Converge* are similar in character and theme to those of the first collection. Such repetitions are occasionally tedious but, on the whole, they serve merely to remind us that the artist—whatever his initial gift—must ultimately discover the bounds of his talent. Flannery O'Connor freely admitted the limitations imposed by such inner necessity. She explained that her characters were consistently grotesque "because it is the nature of my talent to make them so. To some extent, the writer can choose his subject; but he can never choose what he is able to make live." [6] Or, as Proust observes, "Great writers never create but a single work, or rather they consistently refract through different media a single beauty that they bring into the world." [7] The "single beauty" of Flannery O'Connor is stunning indeed.

CHAPTER 10

A Canon Completed

I *Some Objections Answered*

CERTAIN charges are recurrently raised against Flannery O'Connor's work by those who are unsympathetic to her aims. The first criticism—a major one—is that her rigid view of humanity is lacking in sufficient compassion. Certainly, her work affords evidence to support such an accusation; but her intention is always to correct the view of a permissive society which confounds freedom with license and confuses a lax approval with responsible understanding. For those characters who strive to align themselves with something more enduring than "progress," more meaningful than transient involvement in pleasure or property—for Hazel Motes, both Tarwaters, old Tanner, and even the outlaw Rufus—she evinces deep and obvious sympathy. Even in her depictions of those whose limitations beget their own nemesis —the blue-eyed mothers and the guilty sons—we sense in her attitude a concern that comes close to love. Like Swift or Jonson, she castigates man that he may awaken to his folly before it is too late. She is ever on her way to rouse the sleeping city, calling out that every day is "judgement day," a reminder many prefer to ignore.

A second complaint protests the apparent absence in her work of a sense of natural beauty. True, we seldom turn from her creations refreshed by a sense of the transcendental beauty of natural forms. More often, the atmosphere reflects the characters' dispositions—"sour," "dull," "sullen." The landscape—though it seldom reinforces our sense of the esthetic attractions of the surroundings—serves very well its intended purpose: to set the emotional tone of the narrations. Her characters—themselves so frequently marred inwardly or outwardly by self-imposed spiritual deprivation—are for the most part oblivious to the beauties about them. They pay no heed to the stars over Taulkingham or to the peacock's splendor. Mr. Fortune three times moves to the window to discover the mystery of the "view" his granddaughter praises; but, blind to the beauty before him, he matter-of-factly concludes that "a pine trunk is a pine trunk."

The sun itself is the most important element of O'Connor's natural settings, and it is most often employed in one of two typical moments, both of major importance in establishing psychological setting. In the first of these, the sun at midday burns the sky into a brilliant blankness to provide an absolutely neutral backdrop for the dramatic action preparing on the human scene. Such episodes are like sudden shifts into intense black-and-white movie sequences, where the tension of the action is reinforced by the sharp delineation of the characters in closeup. Furthermore, the whitening of the sky—until all clouds are burned away and the sun itself may disappear—suggests a purification and removal of all inconsequential, accidental features of earthly experience into an essential reality where *quality* as defined by human subjectivity no longer obtains. God as pure spirit does not manifest Himself in accidents of color, shape, or texture. He is the essence— the seeming nothingness which remains when all phenomenal accidents have been removed.

Against such radiance, Mrs. May encounters her fatal lover, the grandmother is struck down after her brief moment of grace, and Mrs. Turpin confesses her humiliation to the uncomprehending audience of black helpers. These blazing scenes depict moments of absolute truth, when one at last confronts the undeniable realities of self which he has so long ignored.

A second major emblematic use of the sun occurs when, at sunset, the brilliant reds of the Georgia sky become dramatic reminders of the Passion of the Cross. To the child contemplating the mysteries of divine perfection incarnate in the imperfect human vessel, the sun over the dark woods is "like an elevated Host drenched in blood." Mr. Fortune, viewing the trees "bathed in blood" as if "someone were wounded behind the woods," feels himself held by "an uncomfortable mystery." And Mrs. Turpin, gazing at the crimson curtain of the evening sky, perceives a "vast swinging bridge extending upward from the earth through a field of living fire." The "beauty" of such scenes goes beyond external splendor to reveal the agony by which man joins Christ in the suffering of Calvary.

The natural setting is invariably fitted to the action. Mr. Shiftlet's hypocritic prayer to the Lord to "Break forth and wash the slime from this earth" is voiced beneath an angry, roiling sky. But Mr. Head, returning home to experience a second action of mercy, is met by a scene of delicate moonlit beauty: "the moon, restored to its full splendor, sprang from a cloud and flooded the clearing with light. As they stepped off, the sage grass was shivering gently in shades of silver and the clinkers under their feet glittered with a fresh black light. The treetops, fencing the junction like the protecting walls of a garden, were darker than the sky which was hung with gigantic white clouds illuminated like lanterns."

A third objection, one which is in fact an extension of the other two, is that O'Connor's works are depressing because of her overemphasis on "morbid" and "bizarre" aspects of experience. To this objection, we can only say that Flannery O'Connor is seeking to reach precisely that audience which would resolutely contemplate only the "smiling aspects of life." Like Melville, she insists that the sharks hidden in the depths are as much of the scene as the gilded sea surface which lulls the viewer into a dangerous serenity. Her vision is apocalyptic; and, of those who prefer to shrug off such serious visions of man's destiny, she would doubtless say that they suffer "the blindness of those who don't know that they cannot see."

II An Artist of Her Region

Flannery O'Connor loudly protested the casual dismissal of her work as merely another expression from the "Southern school." She herself observed on this point:

Most readers these days must be sufficiently sick of hearing about Southern writers and Southern writing and what so many reviewers insist upon calling the "Southern school." No one has ever made plain just what the Southern school is or which writers belong to it. Sometimes, when it is most respectable, it seems to mean the little group of Agrarians that flourished at Vanderbilt in the twenties; but more often the term conjures up an image of Gothic monstrosities and the idea of a preoccupation with everything deformed and grotesque. Most of us are considered, I

believe, to be unhappy combinations of Poe and Erskine Caldwell.[1]

Yet, despite her intense protestations, certain elements in her
work link her undeniably with the mainstream of Southern literature both traditional and modern. The frontier writers, in particular, are famed for their vivid couplings of humor with violence
—a trait that has continued to characterize the Southern writer
down to our own age. In Judge Longstreet's sketch "The Fight"
(Georgia Scenes), the audience is titillated by an account of
brutal combat between two frontier strong men, one of whom
gets his nose bitten off by his opponent, who in turn loses a finger
and an ear. In "Mrs. Yardley's Quilting," by George Washington
Harris, hilarity ensues when that lady's prize coverlets are
dragged off the line by a wild horse. The fact that two lives are
lost—those of the hapless rider and the hostess, who expires from
the loss of the diamond quilt and from getting trampled by the
runaway as he leaves—is incidental to the fun.

Mark Twain also mixed the laughable and the terrible: note
such episodes in *Huckleberry Finn* as the Sheperdson-Granger-
ford feud; the Boggs-Sherburn shooting incident; the absurd but
sinister connivings of the Duke and the Dauphin, who turn a
profit by selling Jim back into slavery; and the entire Phelps farm
episode in which this genteel family interrupts its joke making
long enough to chain Jim to a bedstead in a dirt-floor shack out
back, and Tom Sawyer indulges his penchant for medieval fantasy
by putting Jim through a series of rigorous torments before an-
nouncing his emancipation. Twain's awareness of the casual yok-
ing of the absurd and the deplorable in everyday life is epitomized in Huck's offhand answer to Mrs. Phelps's query about
the steamboat wreck ("Anybody hurt?" "No'm. Killed a nigger.")

In our own time, Faulkner in particular is noted for his fre-
quent fusion of violent and comic elements. This trait is amply
illustrated in *The Hamlet* when Mink Snopes murders Jack
Houston and then frantically attempts to dispose of the body.
Mink first laboriously deposits the corpse in a hollow trunk, returning later to retrieve the body with an ax. He then dumps
the cadaver in the river, only to observe that it is disappointingly
minus a limb, which he inadvertently detached in the process of
installing the body in the tree. He returns to the mangled tree

stump and there doggedly probes for the missing member. Throughout the scene, the humor aroused by Flem's furious efforts is leavened by a rising horror at the actual occupation in which he is engaged. The double focus of the grisly comedy parallels the dual thrust of the novel toward the rarefied regions of myth on the one hand and coarse country realism on the other.

Katherine Anne Porter, Erskine Caldwell, Truman Capote, Carson McCullers—all discover a comic residue in disaster. Even Eudora Welty occasionally weds terror and laughter, as in "Clytie," where she leaves her unfortunate heroine up-ended in a rain barrel. The Southerners' irreverent refusal to separate the comic and the catastrophic in airtight compartments lays them open to the chronic charge that they deliberately seek sensational effects. Yet, much of their undeniable success is attributable to their emphatic insistence on the inherent complexity of human experience, one in which comic and tragic moments do not group themselves in orderly arrangement around conveniently isolated poles, but often interfuse and in fact help to establish by their very presence the essential timbre of the antithesis. Likewise in the work of Flannery O'Connor, comedy modulates tragedy, and laughter is tempered by impending disaster.

III An Artist of Her Time

Though her contrapuntal manipulation of comic-serious elements allies Flannery O'Connor closely to many of her regional predecessors and contemporaries, she is assuredly much more than just a "Southern" writer. Her likeness to such figures as Nathanael West and Ring Lardner has been frequently remarked. Indeed, many of her major preoccupations are those which define the main currents of twentieth-century literature. Her concern for violence, for example, is shared by many writers of the last half-century, from Franz Kafka to Alain Robbe-Grillet.

Her acute awareness of the essential absurdity which characterizes much of daily experience finds numerous analogues in Samuel Beckett, Eugene Ionesco, or, in modified form, Albert Camus, who poses the doctrine of the absurd at the center of his ideology. The banal exchanges of O'Connor's characters are frequently like regional renderings of Ionesco's pointless dialogues. But the grotesque mode, traditionally associated with the Southern school, is, in fact, a prominent feature of much of modern American and world literature. Sherwood Anderson, Kafka, Edward Albee are but representatives of the vast group which rely on grotesquerie as a prime instrument in conveying their world vision.

And, although O'Connor's controlled artistry is far removed from the ostensibly unstructured creations of the Surrealists, her drama moves at times surprisingly close to the Surrealistic moment. The unanticipated catastrophe involves a violent dislocation of the normal frame of experience, and the victims seldom find rational explanations to account for the irrational event. Furthermore, the agents and circumstances of the disaster frequently suggest nightmare visions thrown up from the very depths of the unconscious. The homicidal maniac appearing on the horizon above the vacationing family, the son who becomes his mother's inadvertent executioner, the farm trio watching in paralyzed horror as the tractor grinds the helpless Pole to death before their eyes—these seem terrible extensions of a reality gone amuck, the tragic consequence of a sudden collapse of rational structures.

In O'Connor's fiction, we begin invariably in the seemingly "safe" world of the normal and familiar; but we proceed inevitably to the dire moment when the scaffolds of reality collapse into the perilous chaos of the unlooked-for peripety. The consequent fall is not merely from "good fortune" to bad but from rational forms of consciousness into Surrealistic realms where all prior assumptions are challenged and threatened with annihilation. Even the stories of revelation partake of this nonrational aspect. Basically, O'Connor's emphasis on violence and absurdity, her insistence on the grotesque evidence and the Surrealistic moment, fuse in a vision which is simultaneously comic and tragic. This blending of disparate modes to produce a single effect is typical of many modern writers. The choice is not—for these writers or for O'Connor—one of either-or. Life does not seal its subjects into neat categories, easily identifiable for purposes of evoking an appropriate emotional attitude. The serious and the absurd, the laughable and the deplorable, constantly overlap in life—and in the art of the present century.

Finally, Flannery O'Connor participates—whether intentionally or not—in the demonic vision of the century. Her biting irony evokes the devil's laugh. The mysteries she explores permit of nihilistic as well as affirmative explanations. The omnipresent disasters suggest a potentially mechanistic universe in which man is struck down without notice by the blind laws of chance. Assuredly, her conscious intention is to support no such subversive view. But the thrust is clearly discernible, and any evaluation of her total effect must take the demonic impulse into account.

IV "A Realist of Distances"

Despite Flannery O'Connor's affinities with various impulses which distinguish contemporary writing, she is, in other respects, set apart in a category which is virtually unique. The ethos of her vision is, ultimately, medieval rather than modern. She shares with the medieval mind the insistence that reality reposes in abstract mysteries of being rather than in the concrete minutiae of daily experience; hence her fiction tends always toward allegory. Although she works within the traditional frame of literary Realism, with its stress on the particularities of time, place, and sequential action, she is unconcerned with these as meaningful in themselves. Nor is she absorbed with personality as a prime center of interest. Thus, we do not find in her narratives the obsessive probing of sensibility which preoccupies Proust, Virginia Woolf, or Henry James. Likewise, she is unconcerned to delineate "reality" after the manner of the Naturalists through the multiple accumulation of inconsequential detail. Reality, for her, finally resides not in the fact of experience nor in the subjective response to it but in the unchanging categories of truth divorced from transitory expression.

This is not to say, however, that O'Connor emphasizes abstraction to the detriment of particularity. On the contrary, she is a master of the use of the concrete detail to individualize her action, of the art of *showing* as opposed to *telling*. But the profuse concretion of her work points ever toward the level of high abstraction. She demonstrates again and again that the way up is first the way down, that ascension can occur only as the extension of an initially downward path. She would endorse the assertion of William Lynch that "the finite is not itself a generality, to be encompassed in one fell swoop. Rather, it contains many shapes and byways and cleverness and powers and diversities and persons, and we must not go too fast from the many to the one. We waste our time if we try to go around or above or under the definite; we must literally go through it." [2]

As a religious dogmatist, she embraces an established set of values, and she rejects all relativistic efforts to redefine the criteria of judgment. For her, the center of being is God, not man; and she dismisses as absurd humanistic attempts to delineate reality with man-made instruments, or to assess human behavior in terms of a relativistic ethic. She scorns the cult of progress and insists upon the validity of original sin as the source of man's guilt and as the explanation for his faulty behavior. Man is fallen, and all his technological achievements—his automobiles and airplanes and potato peelers—cannot conceal the fact. The modern interpreter's insistence that the Scriptures mean only what he wishes, and that an indiscriminate love is the proper expression of the religious sentiment, cannot negate the examples of the ancient monks in their coffins. She contends that the final realities of Sin, Atonement, and Redemption exist intact. She is, then, an absolutist in an age which has embraced relativism on all levels. Thus, Flannery O'Connor supports the invisible realm against the world of things, the unseen essence as against the objective manifestation. In this respect, her vision is essentially that of another age, and her work is a persistent attempt to recall those formerly accepted truths to the human consciousness once again.

Because of the intricate complexity of her vision, whose diverse elements fuse as "Christian tragicomedy," Flannery O'Connor's works have confused some readers and alienated others who have misunderstood or rejected the aims she seeks. She herself foresaw that her creations might not meet with immediate understanding and acceptance, but she insisted that she was prepared to wait to have her fiction understood, even fifty or a hundred years. She added, "A few readers go a long way if they're the right kind." [3] Fortunately, recognition came sooner than she had foreseen. A *Book Week* panel has described her work as being among "the most distinguished fiction published in America during the years 1945-65." With this evaluation, an ever-expanding audience of the "right kind" of readers would heartily concur.

Notes and References

Preface

1. Quoted by Lewis Lawson, review of *Everything That Rises Must Converge*, *Studies in Short Fiction*, III (Spring, 1966), 376.

Chapter One

1. The stories of her thesis reveal a student of substantial promise, but there is little evidence of the power which was to stamp O'Connor's work so forcefully later on. The situations are fairly commonplace: an old transplanted Southerner is upset by the kindnesses offered him by a Northern black ("The Geranium"); a Southern "liberal" comes into violent disagreement with his barber on the race question ("The Barber"); an old black man waits helpless in his cabin for death to come in the form of a wild animal ("Wildcat"); a sterile female writer tries to live vicariously through her imaginary characters ("The Crop"); two young boys discover for themselves that "might makes right" ("The Turkey"); and a country boy named Haze goes for a ride on the train ("The Train").

2. Disseminated lupus erythematosis is a collagen disease arising when the system produces antibodies which attack its own connective tissues. The term *lupus* (wolf) is applied because the patient frequently manifests a butterfly-shaped rash over the nose, giving his face a "wolflike" appearance. The disease is characterized by progressive physical degeneration. Flannery O'Connor's father died of the same disease when he was forty-five.

3. Quoted by Louis D. Rubin, Jr., "Two Ladies of the South," *Sewanee Review*, LXIII (Autumn, 1955), 677.

4. Margaret Meaders, "Flannery O'Connor: 'Literary Witch,'" *Colorado Quarterly*, X (Spring, 1962), 378.

5. "The Fiction Writer and His Country," *Mystery and Manners*, ed. Sally and Robert Fitzgerald (New York, 1969), p. 27.

6. Unfortunately, this mural was destroyed in a later building program of the school.

7. Meaders, p. 385.

8. Granville Hicks, "A Writer at Home with Her Heritage," *Saturday Review,* XLV (May 12, 1962), 22.
9. Richard Stern, "Flannery O'Connor: A Remembrance and Some Letters," *Shenandoah,* XVI (Winter, 1965), 7.
10. *Ibid.,* p. 5.
11. *Ibid.,* p. 10.
12. C. Ross Mullins, "Flannery O'Connor, An Interview," *Jubilee,* XI (June, 1963), 35.
13. "Replies to Two Questions," *Esprit,* III (Winter, 1959), 10.
14. Katherine Fugin, Faye Rivard, and Margaret Sieh, "An Interview with Flannery O'Connor," *Censer* (Fall, 1960).
15. "The Role of the Catholic Novelist," *Greyfriar,* VII (1964), 7.
16. "The Fiction Writer and His Country," *Mystery and Manners,* p. 29.
17. Quoted by Robert Fitzgerald, Introduction, *Everything That Rises Must Converge,* p. xiii.
18. "The Fiction Writer and His Country," *Mystery and Manners,* p. 32.
19. Mullins, p. 33.
20. "The Fiction Writer and His Country," *Mystery and Manners,* p. 31.
21. "The Church and the Fiction Writer," *Mystery and Manners,* p. 150.
22. "The Fiction Writer and His Country," *Mystery and Manners,* p. 27.
23. Joel Wells, "Off the Cuff," *Critic,* XXI (August-September, 1962), 72.
24. "The Role of the Catholic Novelist," p. 9.
25. Mullins, p. 34.
26. "The Fiction Writer and His Country," *Mystery and Manners,* p. 31.

Chapter Two

1. Gerald E. Sherry, "An Interview with Flannery O'Connor," *Critic,* XXI (June-July, 1963), 29.
2. In his introduction to *Everything That Rises Must Converge,* Robert Fitzgerald reflects: "Has not tragicomedy at least since Dante been the most Christian of *genres?*" (p. xxxiii).
3. Betsy Lochridge, "An Afternoon with Flannery O'Connor," *Atlanta Journal and Atlanta Constitution,* (November 1, 1959).
4. Bob Dowell, "The Moment of Grace in the Fiction of Flannery O'Connor," *College English,* XXVII (December, 1965), 235.
5. For relevant discussion of the grotesque, see Arthur Clayborough,

The Grotesque in English Literature (Oxford, 1965), and Wolfgang Kayser, *The Grotesque in Art and Literature* (New York, 1966).
6. "The Fiction Writer and His Country," *Mystery and Manners*, pp. 33–34.
7. Dowell, p. 239.
8. Meaders, pp. 381–82.
9. Introduction to *A Memoir of Mary Ann, Mystery and Manners*, p. 226.
10. Mullins, p. 33.
11. Introduction to *A Memoir of Mary Ann, Mystery and Manners*, p. 228.
12. Quoted by Fitzgerald, Introduction, *Everything That Rises Must Converge*, pp. xxvii–xxviii.
13. See Karl S. Guthke, *Modern Tragicomedy: An Investigation into the Nature of the Genre* (New York, 1966).
14. "Flannery O'Connor's Devil," *Sewanee Review*, LXX (Summer, 1962), 401.
15. Brainard Cheney, "Miss O'Connor Creates Unusual Humor Out of Ordinary Sin," *Sewanee Review*, LXXI (Autumn, 1963), 644–52.

Chapter Three

1. Anon., "Frustrated Preacher," *Newsweek*, XXXIX (May 19, 1952), 114, unsigned review.
2. Anon., *Time Magazine*, LIX (June 9, 1952), 108, 111, unsigned review.
3. Isaac Rosenfeld, "To Win by Default," *New Republic*, CXXVII (July 7, 1952), 19.
4. Thomas Mann, Preface to the German edition of Joseph Conrad's *The Secret Agent*. Quoted in Karl S. Guthke, *Modern Tragicomedy*, [vii].
5. Robert Fitzgerald, Introduction, *Everything That Rises Must Converge*, p. xvi, states that O'Connor encountered the Oedipus story midway in the composition of *Wise Blood* and rewrote the narrative to build toward Haze's atonement through self-blinding as the climactic act of the novel.
6. Like Haze, Enoch is a country boy come to town. O'Connor has remarked, "Southern cities are full of country people." Sherry, p. 29.
7. Owen Barfield, *Saving the Appearances: A Study in Idolatry* (New York, n.d.), pp. 82–83.
8. "The Novelist and Free Will," *Fresco*, n.s. I (Winter, 1963), 100.

9. Augustine, *The City of God,* trans. Marcus Dods (New York, 1950), p. 477 (Book XV).

10. Walter Hilton, *The Ladder of Perfection,* trans. and intr. Leo Sherley-Price (Harmondsworth, 1957), p. 178.

11. Evelyn Underhill, *Mysticism: A Study in the Development of Man's Spiritual Consciousness* (New York, 1955), p. 205.

12. This remark, along with Haze's explanation to Mrs. Flood that he is acting as he does in order "to pay," clearly establishes the meaning of Haze's final course as a return to God through acts of extreme expiation. Some readers miss these important clues and see in Haze's behavior signs of his continuing allegiance to the godless "Church Without Christ." O'Connor's own comments—quoted at the end of this chapter—should dispel any final doubts as to Haze's intentions.

13. Barfield, p. 163.

14. Readers have frequently speculated as to why O'Connor so frequently chose to write of Protestant rather than Catholic subjects. She explained that the Catholic novelist in the South often discovers a strong feeling of kinship with "those aspects of Southern life where the religious feeling is most intense and where its outward forms are farthest from the Catholic." "The Role of the Catholic Novelist," p. 8.

Chapter Four

1. Similar "either-or" philosophies are expressed by the prophet Hazel Motes; the preacher Bevel Summers ("The River"); and the delinquent Rufus Johnson ("The Lame Shall Enter First").

2. "The Novelist and Free Will," p. 100.

3. Although the term *grace* is subject to many nuances of interpretation, basically it implies (according to the New English Dictionary) "the free and unmerited favor of God as manifested in the salvation of sinners."

4. See "Everything That Rises Must Converge," "The Comforts of Home," "Greenleaf," and "Judgement Day" for various developments of this theme.

Chapter Five

1. Quoted by Fitzgerald, Introduction, *Everything That Rises Must Converge,* p. xxiv.

2. Quoted by Meaders, p. 384.

3. Mr. Paradise shares certain obvious affinities with the lavender-shirted rapist of *The Violent Bear It Away.* In O'Connor's works, sexual depravity is frequently used to reflect spiritual corruption: witness Manley Pointer, Sabbath Lily Hawks, Leora Watts, and others. For a discussion of O'Connor's "Jansenist" views of sex, see

Warren Coffey, "Flannery O'Connor," *Commentary,* XL (November, 1965), 93–99.

4. "The Novelist and Free Will," p. 100.

5. "An Interview with Flannery O'Connor," *Censer,* Fall, 1960.

6. "The Role of the Catholic Novelist," p. 11.

7. For a full discussion of transformation symbolism in the mass, see C. G. Jung, *Psyche and Symbol* (New York, 1958), pp. 148–225.

8. See Jung, p. 168.

9. "The Church and the Fiction Writer," *Mystery and Manners,* p. 146.

10. For O'Connor's comments on the role of the hitchhiker, see "An Interview with Flannery O'Connor and Robert Penn Warren," *Writer to Writer,* Floyd C. Watkins and Karl F. Knight, eds. (Boston, 1966), pp. 87–88.

11. The Schlitz Playhouse presented a television version of "The Life You Save." O'Connor said of this performance: "I didn't recognize the television version. Gene Kelly played Mr. Shiftlet and for the idiot daughter they got some young actress who had just been voted one of the ten most beautiful women in the world, and they changed the ending just a bit by having Shiftlet suddenly get a conscience and come back for the girl." Wells, p. 72.

Chapter Six

1. The title of the second novel is taken from Matthew 11:12: "From the days of John the Baptist until now the kingdom of heaven suffereth violence and the violent bear it away." Robert McCown suggests that, for Flannery O'Connor, "the 'violent' are those who by their lives and utterances plant the kingdom of God in the hearts of others." "The Education of a Prophet," *Kansas Magazine,* 1962, p. 73.

2. On Tarwater's role as a non-Catholic, O'Connor observed: "I'm not interested in the sects as sects; I'm concerned with the religious individual, the backwoods prophet." Granville Hicks, "A Writer at Home with Her Heritage," *Saturday Review,* XLV (May 12, 1962), 22. In a letter to Sister Mariella Gable, she said: "Old Tarwater is not typical of the Southern Baptist or the Southern Methodist. Essentially he's a crypto-Catholic. When you leave a man alone with his Bible and the Holy Ghost inspires him, he's going to be a Catholic one way or another, even though he knows nothing of the visible Church." Sister Mariella Gable, "Ecumenic Core in the Fiction of Flannery O'Connor," *American Benedictine Review,* XV (June, 1964), 134.

3. Speaking of Hawthorne, O'Connor said, "I am one of his descendants." Letter to William Sessions. Reprinted in *The Added Dimension,* ed. Melvin J. Friedman and Lewis A. Lawson (New

York, 1966), p. 223. She also reveals strong affinities with Nathanael West, Ring Lardner, Gogol, Poe, Faulkner, and T. S. Eliot, all of whom she had read. In addition, her name has been linked with Blake, Kafka, Truman Capote, and Mary Lavin.

4. Wells, p. 72.

5. O'Connor's continuing concern for the "mistake of nature" is revealed also in her Introduction to *A Memoir of Mary Ann*, where she discusses the problem as presented in Hawthorne's "The Birth Mark." O'Connor, like Hawthorne, insists upon man's obligation to accept—and love—his fellow human beings, even when they manifest depressing tokens of human imperfection.

6. This situation occurs in slightly modified form in "The River." Likewise, both stories depict the extreme of spiritual depravity through the character of a sexual degenerate, and they strongly imply that it is better to die into a pure world of spirit than risk contamination by the corruptions of a physical earth.

7. Dante and Milton also associate noxious odors with moral decay.

8. On her use of the devil, O'Connor commented: "In the Gospels it was the devils who first recognized Christ, and the evangelists didn't censor this information. They apparently thought it was pretty good witness. It scandalizes us when we see the same thing in modern dress only because we have this defensive attitude toward the faith." Gable, p. 141.

9. O'Connor explained that she permitted the devil to deliver his arguments in person because: "I want to be certain that the devil gets identified as the devil and not simply taken as this or that psychological tendency." Gable, p. 132.

10. Some readers object to the rape episode as superfluous to the action. O'Connor observes: "In my stories a reader will find that the devil accomplishes a good deal of ground work that seems to be necessary before grace is effective. Tarwater's final vision could not have been brought off if he hadn't met the man in the lavender and cream-colored car. This is another mystery." "The Novelist and Free Will," p. 101.

Chapter Seven

1. The girl's name—Mary Grace—is significant: the first part links her with the purity of the Virgin; the second suggests her role as the divine agent by whom Mrs. Turpin is brought to grace.

2. Mrs. Turpin's visual dislocation suggests an interesting parallel with O'Connor's view of the "prophetic role" of the fiction writer: "In the novelist's case, it is a matter of seeing near things with their

extensions of meaning and thus of seeing far things close up." "The Role of the Catholic Novelist," p. 9.

3. Underhill, p. 275.

4. Both are names of unmistakable Old Testament origin. Obadiah ("worshiper of Jehovah") appears in the chapter named for him as a prophet of disaster. A later Obadiah is godfearing servant to the godless Ahab. Elihu ("whose God is he") appears before Job to defend the justice of God, who commands the righteous to "return from iniquity."

5. Underhill, pp. 180–81.

Chapter Eight

1. Three of the stories in the thesis focus on the black man or on the problem of race relations. In "Wildcat," Flannery O'Connor attempts for the first and last time the use of a black man as the point-of-view character.

2. Flannery O'Connor named "The Artificial Nigger" as her favorite among her stories. Wells, p. 72.

3. In "An Interview with Flannery O'Connor and Robert Penn Warren," O'Connor explains the origin of the title: When her mother asked a countryman on the side of the road where a house was, he said, " 'Well, you go into this town, and you can't miss it 'cause it's the only house in town with a artificial nigger in front of it.' So I decided I would have to find a story to fit that." *Writer to Writer*, p. 73.

4. In "The Novelist and Free Will," O'Connor refers to "what the artificial nigger does to reunite Mr. Head and Nelson" as "the working of grace."

5. For further discussion of the peacock's symbolic function, see Sister M. Joselyn, "Thematic Centers in 'The Displaced Person,' " *Studies in Short Fiction*, I (Winter, 1964), 85–92.

6. Louis Rubin discusses the theme of displacement in the story in "Two Ladies of the South," *Sewanee Review*, LXIII (Autumn, 1955), 671–81. Another excellent analysis is Robert Fitzgerald's "The Countryside and the True Country," *Sewanee Review*, LXX (Summer, 1962), 380–94.

7. However, we may assume that O'Connor, along with De Chardin, sees the many convergences as necessary traumas in the ascent to higher levels of being.

8. Cf. Julian's mother and the black woman in "Everything That Rises."

9. Mullins, pp. 33–34.

Chapter Nine

1. Robert Ardrey (*The Territorial Imperative*: New York, 1966), posits the notion that attachment to property is the key human characteristic, overriding concern for sex, food, spiritual satisfaction, and so forth. To some extent, Flannery O'Connor's observations on human nature would seem to support his assertions, though she, of course, deplores man's excessive attachment to things.

2. O'Connor herself was fully aware of the danger that the artist might, in fact, fall into sterile repetitions: "I'm afraid it is possible to exhaust your material. What you exhaust are those things that you are capable of bringing alive." Mullins, p. 35.

3. C. S. Lewis, *Christian Behavior* (London, 1943), pp. 29–30.

4. Edmund Bergler advances this view. See Leonard Feinberg, *The Satirist* (New York, 1964), pp. 217–21.

5. "He [the average Catholic reader] forgets that sentimentality is an excess, a distortion of sentiment usually in the direction of an overemphasis on innocence, and that innocence, whenever it is overemphasized in the ordinary human condition, tends by some natural law to become its opposite." "The Church and the Fiction Writer," *Mystery and Manners*, pp. 147–48.

6. Quoted by James J. Farnham, "The Grotesque in Flannery O'Connor," *America* (May 13, 1961), p. 277.

7. Quoted in Feinberg, p. 85.

Chapter Ten

1. "The Fiction Writer and His Country," *Mystery and Manners*, p. 28.

2. William Lynch, *Christ and Apollo: The Dimensions of the Literary Imagination* (New York, 1963), p. 23.

3. Meaders, p. 383.

Selected Bibliography

PRIMARY SOURCES

1. Novels and Collected Stories:

Wise Blood. New York: Harcourt, Brace and Co., 1952.

A Good Man Is Hard to Find and Other Stories. New York: Harcourt, Brace, World and Co., 1955. (Stories appear within the volume in the following order. Place of original publication is indicated.)

"A Good Man Is Hard to Find," *Modern Writing I,* ed. William Phillips and Philip Rahv. New York, 1953, pp. 186–99.

"The River," *Sewanee Review,* LXI (Summer, 1953), 455–75.

"The Life You Save May Be Your Own," *Kenyon Review,* XV (Spring, 1953), 195–207.

"A Stroke of Good Fortune," *Shenandoah,* IV (Spring, 1953), 7–18. (Originally published as "The Woman on the Stairs," *Tomorrow,* VIII (August, 1949), 40.)

"A Temple of the Holy Ghost," *Harper's Bazaar,* LXXXVIII (May, 1954), 108–9, 162–64.

"The Artificial Nigger," *Kenyon Review,* XVII (Spring, 1955), 169–92.

"A Circle in the Fire," *Kenyon Review,* XVI (Spring, 1954), 169–90.

"A Late Encounter with the Enemy," *Harper's Bazaar,* LXXXVII (September, 1953), 234, 247, 249, 252.

"Good Country People," *Harper's Bazaar,* LXXXIX (June, 1955), 64–5, 116–17, 121–22, 124, 130.

"The Displaced Person," *Sewanee Review,* LXII (October, 1954), 634–54.

The Violent Bear It Away. New York: Farrar, Straus and Cudahy, 1960.

Everything That Rises Must Converge. New York: Farrar, Straus and Giroux, 1965. (Stories appear within the volume in the following order. Place of original publication is indicated.)

"Everything That Rises Must Converge," *New World Writing*, XIX (1961), 74–90.

"Greenleaf," *Kenyon Review*, XVIII (Summer, 1956), 384–410.

"A View of the Woods," *Partisan Review*, XXIV (Fall, 1957), 475–96.

"The Enduring Chill," *Harper's Bazaar*, XC (July, 1958), 44–5, 94, 96, 100–102, 108.

"The Comforts of Home," *Kenyon Review*, XXII (Fall, 1960), 523–54.

"The Lame Shall Enter First," *Sewanee Review*, LXX (Summer, 1962), 337–79.

"Revelation," *Sewanee Review*, LXXII (Spring, 1964), 178–202.

"Parker's Back," *Esquire*, LXIII (April, 1965), 76–78, 151–55.

"Judgement Day" (previously unpublished).

The Complete Stories of Flannery O'Connor. New York: Farrar, Straus and Giroux, 1971. (Contains the nineteen previously collected stories plus the following. Place of original publication is indicated.)

"The Geranium," *Accent*, VI (Summer, 1946), 245–53. (From thesis.)

"The Barber," *Atlantic*, CCXXVI (October, 1970), 111–12, 116–18. (From thesis.)

"Wildcat," *North American Review*, VII (Spring, 1970), 66–68. (From thesis.)

"The Crop," *Mademoiselle*, LXXII (April, 1971), 216–17, 273–75. (From thesis.)

"The Turkey." Published as "The Capture," *Mademoiselle*, XXVIII (November, 1948), 20–23, 82–85. (From thesis.)

"Train," *Sewanee Review*, LVI (April, 1948), 261–71. (From thesis. Later incorporated into *Wise Blood*.)

"The Peeler," *Partisan Review*, XVI (December, 1949), 1189–1206. (Incorporated into *Wise Blood*.)

"The Heart of the Park," *Partisan Review*, XVI (February, 1949), 138–51. (Incorporated into *Wise Blood*.)

"Enoch and the Gorilla," *New World Writing*, I (April, 1952), 67–74. (Incorporated into *Wise Blood*.)

"You Can't Be Any Poorer Than Dead," *New World Writing*, VIII (October, 1955), 81–97. (Incorporated into *The Violent Bear It Away*.)

"The Partridge Festival," *Critic*, XIX (February-March, 1961), 20–23, 82–85.

"Why Do the Heathens Rage?," *Esquire*, LX (July, 1963), 60–61. (From an untitled projected novel.)

2. Articles, Addresses, and Reviews:

Mystery and Manners; Occasional Prose. Ed. Sally and Robert Fitz-
gerald. New York: Farrar, Straus and Giroux, 1969. (Includes
several "composites" plus the following previously published
articles.)
"The King of the Birds." Published as "Living with a Peacock,"
Holiday, XXX (September, 1961), 52–53, 55.
"The Fiction Writer and His Country." *The Living Novel, a Sym-
posium.* Ed. Granville Hicks. New York: Macmillan, 1957.
"Some Aspects of the Grotesque in Southern Literature," *Cluster
Review* [Mercer University, Macon, Georgia], Seventh Issue
(March, 1965), 5–6, 22.
"The Regional Writer," *Esprit* [University of Scranton, Scanton,
Pennsylvania], VII (Winter, 1963), 31–35.
"Total Effect and the Eighth Grade." Published as "Fiction Is a
Subject with a History—It Should Be Taught That Way," *Geor-
gia Bulletin,* March 21, 1963, p.l. Book Supplement.
"The Church and the Fiction Writer," *America,* XCVI (March 30,
1957), 733–35.
Introduction. *A Memoir of Mary Ann.* New York: Farrar, Straus
and Cudahy, 1961, pp. 3–21. See also "Mary Ann: An Excerpt
from *A Memoir of Mary Ann,*" *Jubilee,* IX (May, 1961), 28–35.
"Replies to Two Questions," *Esprit,* III (Winter, 1959), 10.
Review of *The Phenomenon of Man, American Scholar,* XXX (Fall,
1961), 618.
"The Role of the Catholic Novelist," *Greyfriar* [Siena College, Lou-
donville, New York], VII (1964), 5–12.

3. Letters and Interviews:

"A Correspondence." [Letters to William Sessions.] Published in
Friedman, Melvin J., and Lewis A. Lawson, eds. *The Added Di-
mension.* New York: Fordham University Press, 1966, pp. 209–25.
Fugin, Katherine, Faye Rivard, and Margaret Sieh. "An Interview
with Flannery O'Connor," *Censer* [College of Saint Teresa,
Winona, Minnesota], (Fall, 1960). Some significant comment
by O'Connor.
"An Interview with Flannery O'Connor and Robert Penn Warren,"
The Vagabond [Vanderbilt University, Nashville, Tennessee],
IV (February, 1960), 9–16. Reprinted in *Writer to Writer.* Ed.
Floyd C. Watkins and Karl F. Knight. Boston: Houghton Mif-
flin, 1966, pp. 71–90. Recorded panel on writers and writing.

Mullins, C. Ross. "Flannery O'Connor: An Interview," *Jubilee*, XI (June, 1963), 32–35. Significant answers to questions on such topics as race relations, Catholic as writer, and so on.

Recent Southern Fiction: A Panel Discussion. Bulletin of Wesleyan College [Macon, Georgia], XLI (January, 1961). O'Connor comments on her life and art.

Sherry, Gerard E. "An Interview with Flannery O'Connor," *Critic,* XXI (June-July, 1963), 29–31. Conversation on diverse topics from the experimental novel to the Southerner in the city.

Stern, Richard. "Flannery O'Connor: A Remembrance and Some Letters," *Shenandoah,* XVI (Winter, 1965), 5–10. Reveals a side of O'Connor seldom seen in her formal writings.

Wells, Joel. "Off the Cuff," *Critic,* XXI (August-September, 1962), 4–5, 71–72. Comments on the Catholic writer and the Protestant audience.

Wylder, J. "Flannery O'Connor: A Reminiscence and Some Letters," *North American Review,* VII (Spring, 1970), 58–65. A further revelation of O'Connor's views.

SECONDARY SOURCES

ALICE, SISTER MARY, O.P. "My Mentor: Flannery O'Connor," *Saturday Review,* XLVIII (May 29, 1965), 24–25. Recollections of a devoted "pupil."

ASALS, FREDERICK. "Flannery O'Connor's 'The Lame Shall Enter First,'" *Mississippi Quarterly,* XXIII (Spring, 1970), 103–20. Focuses on language and imagery to show O'Connor's preoccupation with grotesque perversions of natural forces.

BAUMBACH, JONATHAN. *The Landscape of Nightmare: Studies in the Contemporary American Novel.* New York: New York University Press, 1965, pp. 87–100. Includes close study of *Wise Blood.*

BRITTAIN, JOAN T. "Flannery O'Connor: A Bibliography," *Bulletin of Bibliography,* XXV (1967), 98–100, 123–24, 142.

BURNS, STUART L. "Flannery O'Connor's Literary Apprenticeship," *Renascence,* XXII (Autumn, 1969), 3–16. Examines six early stories to find their relationship to the later masterpieces.

CHENEY, BRAINARD. "Miss O'Connor Creates Unusual Humor Out of Ordinary Sin," *Sewanee Review,* LXXI (Autumn, 1963), 644–52. A refutation of Hawkes's charges of diabolism in O'Connor.

COFFEY, WARREN. "Flannery O'Connor," *Commentary,* XL (November, 1965), 93–99. Attributes O'Connor's sexual puritanism to her Jansenist background.

DRAKE, ROBERT. *Flannery O'Connor: A Critical Essay,* Contemporary Writers in Christian Perspective. Grand Rapids, Michigan: M. B.

Eerdmans Publishing Co., 1966. A useful discussion of O'Connor's Christian concerns.

EFFENSCHWILER, DAVID. "Flannery O'Connor's True and False Prophets," *Renascence*, XXI (Spring, 1969), 151–61, 167. Insists that in *The Violent Bear It Away* O'Connor explores conflicting religious impulses within the main characters.

Esprit. [University of Scranton, Scranton, Pennsylvania], VIII (Winter, 1964). A memorial issue devoted to praise of O'Connor's work by distinguished contributors.

FITZGERALD, ROBERT. "The Countryside and the True Country," *Sewanee Review*, LXX (Summer, 1962), 380–94. Excellent analysis of "The Displaced Person."

———. Introduction. *Everything That Rises Must Converge*. New York: Farrar, Straus and Giroux, 1965. Best biographical portrait of O'Connor. Written by a close friend who is now her literary executor.

FRIEDMAN, MELVIN J. and LEWIS A. LAWSON, eds. *The Added Dimension*. New York: Fordham University Press, 1966. An invaluable collection. Contains perceptive essays by various writers, abundant quotation from O'Connor's nonfiction writings, extensive bibliography.

GORDON, CAROLINE. "Flannery O'Connor's *Wise Blood*," *Critique*, II (Fall, 1958), 3–10. Interesting study of the novel by an early supporter.

GOSSETT, LOUISE Y. *Violence in Recent Southern Fiction*. Durham: Duke University Press, 1965, pp. 75–97. Excellent chapter on O'Connor.

HAWKES, JOHN. "Flannery O'Connor's Devil," *Sewanee Review*, LXX (Summer, 1962), 395–407. Finds O'Connor's attitude "diabolic" as well as "holy."

HENDIN, JOSEPHINE. *The World of Flannery O'Connor*. Bloomington: Indiana University Press, 1970. Contends that O'Connor's assertions of Christian orthodoxy do not accurately describe her art, which derives its strength from an overpowering rage at the world about her.

HICKS, GRANVILLE. "A Cold, Hard Look at Humankind," *Saturday Review*, XLVIII (May 29, 1965), 24–25. Discovers almost no compassion in stories of second collection.

———. "A Writer at Home with Her Heritage," *Saturday Review*, XLV (May 12, 1962), 22–23. An interview with O'Connor.

HYMAN, STANLEY EDGAR. *Flannery O'Connor*. University of Minnesota Pamphlets on American Writers. No. 54. Minneapolis: University of Minnesota Press, 1966. Considers her work in its entirety. Especially useful discussion of major images.

LAWSON, LEWIS A. "Flannery O'Connor and the Grotesque: *Wise Blood*," *Renascence*, XVII (Spring, 1965), 137–47, 156. Useful study of first novel.

LORCH, THOMAS M. "Flannery O'Connor, Christian Allegorist," *Critique*, X (Spring, 1968), 69–80. Finds that O'Connor made extensive use of Christian allegory, especially in the two novels and "The Lame Shall Enter First."

MALE, ROY R. "The Two Versions of 'The Displaced Person,'" *Studies in Short Fiction*, VII (Summer, 1970), 450–57. Compares differences in technique and ultimate impact of first and final published versions.

MARTIN, CARTER W. *The True Country: Themes in the Fiction of Flannery O'Connor*. Nashville: Vanderbilt University Press, 1969. Stresses the importance of O'Connor's sacramental vision.

McCOWN, ROBERT M., S.J. "The Education of a Prophet: A Study of Flannery O'Connor's *The Violent Bear It Away*," *Kansas Magazine* [Kansas State College of Agriculture and Applied Science, Manhattan, Kansas], (1962), pp. 73–78. O'Connor said that McCown "seemed to understand everything I did about the book."

MEADERS, MARGARET INMAN. "Flannery O'Connor: 'Literary Witch,'" *Colorado Quarterly*, X (Spring, 1962), 377–85. An intriguing portrait of O'Connor as a young woman in Milledgeville.

MONTGOMERY, MARION. "Miss Flannery's 'Good Man,'" *Denver Quarterly*, III (Autumn, 1968), 1–17. Reveals that the final scene of "A Good Man Is Hard to Find" is a black confessional, with the grandmother in the role of priest, and the Misfit as penitent.

MURRAY, JAMES G. "Southland á la Russe," *Critic*, XXI (June-July, 1963), 26–28. Excellent discussion of the "display of opposites" in O'Connor's work.

RECHNITZ, ROBERT M. "Passionate Pilgrim: Flannery O'Connor's *Wise Blood*," *Georgia Review*, XIX (Fall, 1965), 310–16. Perceptive interpretation of Hazel Motes's role.

REITER, ROBERT E., ed. *Flannery O'Connor*, The Christian Critic Series. St. Louis, Missouri: B. Herder Book Co., 1968. Excellent collection of previously published critical essays.

ROSENFELD, ISAAC. Review of *Wise Blood*, *New Republic*, CXXVII (July 7, 1952), 19. Finds the novel deficient in execution.

RUBIN, LOUIS D., JR. "Flannery O'Connor: A Note on Literary Fashions," *Critique*, II (Fall, 1958), 11–18. Defends O'Connor against charge that her reputation rests on literary fashion.

————. "Two Ladies of the South," *Sewanee Review*, LXIII (Autumn, 1955), 671–81. Themes and methods in *A Good Man Is Hard To Find*.

STEPHENS, MARTHA. "Flannery O'Connor and the Sanctified Sinner Tradition," *Arizona Quarterly*, XXIV (Autumn, 1968), 223–39. Shows how O'Connor's fiction relates to the work of other contemporary Catholic and Anglo-Catholic writers, notably Graham Greene, T. S. Eliot, and François Mauriac.

TROWBRIDGE, CLINTON W. "The Symbolic Vision of Flannery O'Connor: Patterns of Imagery in *The Violent Bear It Away*," *Sewanee Review*, LXXVI (Spring, 1968), 298–318. Shows how the parable of the loaves and the fishes acts as the controlling image of the novel.

VAN DE KIEFT, RUTH M. "Judgment in the Fiction of Flannery O'Connor," *Sewanee Review*, LXXVI (Spring, 1968), 337–56. Asserts that the apparent cruelty involved in most of O'Connor's endings cannot be termed sadistic, because of her vision of death as revelation.

Index